THE GARDEN LOVER'S GUIDE TO

Italy

THE GARDEN LOVER'S GUIDE TO

Italy

PENELOPE HOBHOUSE
in association with Giorgio Galletti

PRINCETON ARCHITECTURAL PRESS

First published in the United States in 1998 by
Princeton Architectural Press
37 East 7th Street
New York, NY 10003
212.995.9620

For a free catalog of other books published by Princeton Architectural Press,
call toll free 1.800.722.6657 or visit www.papress.com

First published in Great Britain in 1998 by Mitchell Beazley, an imprint
of Reed Consumer Books Limited, London

Library of Congress Cataloging-in-Publication Data for this title is
available upon request from the publisher.

ISBN 1-56898-130-9

For Mitchell Beazley
Executive Editor: Guy Croton
Executive Art Editor: Ruth Hope
Editor: Michèle Byam
Designer: Terry Hirst
Editorial Assistant: Anna Nicholas
Illustrator: Sue Sharples
Cartographer: Kevin Jones
Picture Researcher: Anna Kobryn
Production: Rachel Staveley

For Princeton Architectural Press
Project Coordinator: Mark Lamster
Cover Design: Sara E. Stemen
Special thanks: Eugenia Bell, Caroline Green, Clare Jacobson, Therese
Kelly, and Annie Nitschke – Kevin C. Lippert, *publisher.*

Half title page: Villa Serbelloni, Lake Como
Title: Villa Mansi, Lucca
Contents: Villa d'Este, Tivoli

Printed in Singapore

02 01 00 99 98 5 4 3 2 1 First Edition

Contents

How to use this book **6**

Foreword **7**

Introduction **8**

Lake Como, Lake Maggiore &
the North West **12**

Lake Garda, the Veneto & the North East **42**

Tuscany & the Marches **58**

Rome & its Environs **90**

The South: Sicily & Naples **118**

Glossary and Biographies **140–141**

Index **141**

Acknowledgements **144**

How to use this book

This guide is intended for travellers who wish to visit the most historic and beautiful gardens of Italy. The book is divided into five chapters covering five major regions of Italy. Each chapter comprises an introductory section with a regional map and a list of the gardens, followed by entries on each of the gardens. The entries are accompanied by detailed at-a-glance information telling the reader about the garden's defining characteristics and nearby sights of interest. The guide also includes five "feature" gardens, specially illustrated by three-dimensional plans.

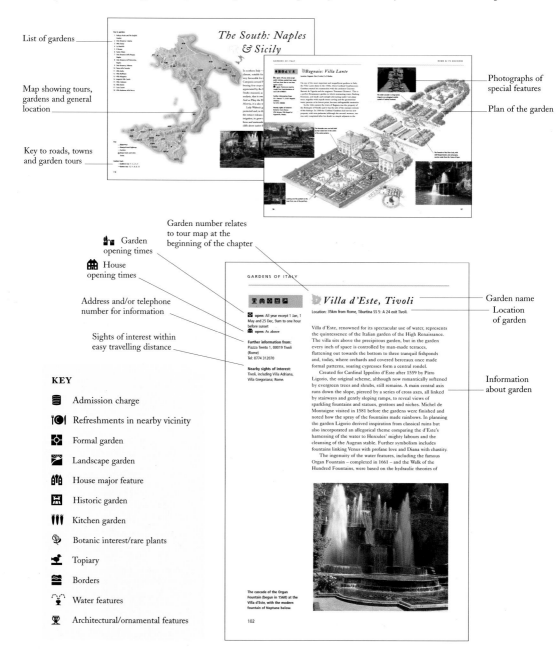

List of gardens

Map showing tours, gardens and general location

Key to roads, towns and garden tours

Photographs of special features

Plan of the garden

Garden number relates to tour map at the beginning of the chapter

Garden opening times

House opening times

Address and/or telephone number for information

Sights of interest within easy travelling distance

Garden name

Location of garden

Information about garden

KEY

🗄 Admission charge

🍴 Refreshments in nearby vicinity

❖ Formal garden

🏞 Landscape garden

🏠 House major feature

🏛 Historic garden

🌿 Kitchen garden

🌷 Botanic interest/rare plants

🦆 Topiary

🗂 Borders

⚱ Water features

♔ Architectural/ornamental features

The cascade of the Organ Fountain (begun in 1568) at the Villa d'Este, with the modern fountain of Neptune below.

Foreword

Gardens in Italy, although in my opinion the most
exciting and historically important in the world, have in
the past been difficult to visit, being either deeply
private or having somewhat eccentric opening hours. On
top of this, for many years the Italian nation appeared to
be neglecting this great heritage. Today things are
different and many of the greatest gardens are regularly
accessible and have been or are being restored with
loving care and authenticity. This has made the task of
choosing over a hundred first-class gardens much easier,
although some of the best can still only be seen by
appointment. Giorgio Galletti, the architect responsible
for the restoration of the Medici gardens in Florence,
has been my guide and has written some entries.

Some gardens are in the book for their historical
significance – their influence on the world development
of gardening. Other gardens have superb plant
collections. A few are even comparatively new and
enthusiastic to share their garden-making with the
interested public.

**Rhododendrons and ferns
border a pool in the Hruska
Botanic Garden on the
western shore of Lake Garda.**

Introduction

Nowadays, almost nothing remains of the Italian gardens made between the decline of the Roman Empire in the 5th century and the 15th and 16th century Renaissance gardens, although the latter still retain an outline of their original layout. Most of those that survive have gone through so many changes that they now exist as layers of history, reflecting five centuries of gardening styles and development. At the end of the 18th and throughout the 19th century some of the most beautiful Italian gardens were transformed into English-style parks. Often it is the best maintained gardens that have suffered most from changing tastes. Influential gardens, such as Pratolino outside Florence, have virtually disappeared, while another famous garden, the Prince Doria in Genoa, faces a motorway, and the greatest of 17th-century gardens, the Villa Venaria Reale in Turin, is now derelict. Fortunately, many other gardens have been sensitively restored: Villa Barbarigo at Valzanzibio, the terraces of Villa Bozzolo della Porta near Lake

The formal parterres or labyrinth, marked out by high hedges of box behind St Peter's Basilica in the Vatican Gardens in Rome.

Maggiore, Cetinale near Siena under Lord Lambton, the Medici Gardens in Florence, and the elaborate waterworks and planting of the Villa d'Este at Tivoli.

It is from the great gardens of the Italian Renaissance that we can learn the principles of classic garden design. It is in these gardens that we learn how garden "rooms" are aligned with the main dwelling, how axes and cross axes can dissect space, how terracing with linking steps and ramps acquire symmetry and proportion on the steepest slopes, and how a garden view can be totally controlled while bringing nature into the garden by expanding its horizons and matching "art with nature". This basic formula, derived from classical Roman precepts, still dictates design rules and the Italian Renaissance villas of the 15th and 16th centuries were inspired by the Roman ideal of life in the country.

During the early 16th century architects were busy incorporating ancient classical statues into gardens. Bramante, through his design for the Cortile del Belvedere in Rome for Pope Julius II (1503), dictated the basis of western European garden design for the next two centuries.

The statue of Atlas and his globe in the central niche of the *nymphaeum* behind Villa Aldobrandini in Frascati.

Tulips and forget-me-nots on the terraces at Villa Carlotta on Lake Como.

The late 17th-century Baroque gardens linked the ordered garden to the wilder landscape, with boundaries between art and nature becoming less distinct, as at Cetinale, Villa Borghese, and Isola Bella on Lake Maggiore. By the early 18th century the initiative in garden design came from France, and French influence is seen in gardens such as Villa Pisani at Strà, Caserta outside Naples, Stupinigi south of Turin, and Villa Belgiojoso near Lecco. In the French-style gardens parterres of broderie were substituted for the geometrically hedged Italian flowerbeds. By the end of the 17th century the English landscape – the *giardino inglese* – became fashionable, often at the cost of older layouts being abandoned, although today many beautiful parks are evidence of their horticultural success. Giuseppe Japelli, the neo-classical architect, developed English gardens throughout northern Italy in the early 19th century.

Although the first botanic teaching gardens were established at Padua and Pisa in 1545, and many new plant species were introduced from the Middle East and the New World during the Renaissance period, these remained subservient to spatial and geometric ideals. Native evergreen oaks, cypresses, bay, and box were part of an overall layout and provided shade, while individual owners expressed their love of flowers and scent and their interest in exotic bulbs and flowers.

Despite the fact that Italy is one of the hottest countries in Europe, its climate has huge variations in temperature. Around the northern lakes and the coastal regions of Liguria, as well as in Naples and Sicily, mild winters make experimental planting of sub-tropical and tropical species possible. However, in central Tuscany the Apennines bring harsh winters so that growing conditions are controlled by altitude and exposure.

The Orto Botanico in Palermo, Sicily, contains many unusual tropical plants and trees.

Key to gardens

1 Castello di Agliè
2 La Mortola
3 Villa Bagatti Valsecchi
4 Villa Balbianello
5 Villa Brivio-Sforza
6 Villa Carlotta
7 Villa Cicogna Mozzoni
8 Villa Cipressi
9 Villa d'Este

10 Villa Melzi
11 Villa Monastero
12 Villa Pizzo
13 Villa Serbelloni
14 Villa Sommi-Picenardi
15 Villa Durazzo Pallavicini
16 Villa Grimaldi
17 Isola Bella
18 Isola Madre

19 Villa della Porta Bozzolo
20 Villa Pallavicino
21 Villa San Remigio
22 Villa Taranto-Ente
23 Villa Negrotto
24 Villa Reale
25 Parco Serra di Comago
26 Villa Sorra
27 Palazzina di Stupinigi

Key

═══ Motorways
─── Principal trunk highways
③ Gardens
🔴 Major towns and cities
● Towns

Garden tours

─── Lake Como tour: 9, 12, 4, 6, 3, 13, 10
─── Lake Maggiore tour: 21, 22, 20, 18, 17, 19

Lake Como, Lake Maggiore & the North West

The northern boundary of Italy is the Alps, below which, and sheltered by the mountains, the Italian lakes, with a high rainfall and with both summer and winter temperatures modified by the expanse of water, provide almost perfect growing conditions for exotic trees and shrubs from many parts of the world. Gardens such as Villa Taranto on Lake Maggiore (p.37), with a high rainfall and hot summers, amply demonstrate the growth potential, with their expansive plantings of a whole range of species. On the Italian Riviera, sheltered by the Ligurian Apennines, microclimatic conditions are even more favourable for plants of Mediterranean type, which will thrive with a comparatively low rainfall and with great summer heat, doing all their growing during the cooler and wetter winter months. At the Giardini Hanbury (p.17), begun in 1867, planting on the steep slopes leading down to the sea takes advantage of the protected site to enable a very wide range of

The Chinese Pagoda that decorates the lake at Villa Durazzo Pallavicini near Genoa.

exotics to succeed and native plants, threatened in the surrounding countryside, to be cherished. Inland, in Piedmont and Lombardy, and in the valley of the River Po and its tributaries, cold winds from the Alps ensure low mean winter temperatures, followed by very hot summers which restrict the plant range.

Although a few early and late Renaissance gardens remain from the 16th and 17th century – such as Cicogna Mozzoni near Varese (p.20–21) and Il Bozzolo della Porta near Laveno (p.35) – in the main the historic gardens of the north, owned by the Austrian Hapsburgs after 1705, were influenced by the fashionable French styles, and often by the 19th century were developed as landscape parks. Gardens such as Stupinigi near Turin (p.41) are essentially French rather than Italian, with avenue axes reaching into the countryside. On Lake Como gardening traditions stretch back into Roman times when Pliny the Younger had two villas beside the lake, known as Comedy and Tragedy.

Distant mountains are reflected in the *Lacus Larius* (the Larian Lake) as Lake Como was known to the Romans. Today many of the splendid lakeside villas, with romantic water landings making Claudian compositions, emphasize the utopian settings. Mostly built between the 16th and 19th centuries, these homes share a style and elegance that is wonderfully reflected in the verdant grounds that surround them. In the landscape-style parks inland from the lakes, there is a more continental climate so that trees, such as the fine oriental plane at Sommi-Picenardi (p.27) and many American specimens at Villa Brivio-Sforza (p.19), grow to vast proportions.

The great water staircase at the Villa Cicogna-Mozzoni Lake Como, flanked by cypresses, leads to a belvedere on the hillside above the lake.

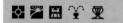

At the Castello di Agliè, the formal parterre gardens below the main buildings are enclosed by high walls.

Castello di Agliè

Location: 30km (18½ miles) N of Turin

As we glide through the poplar plantations and plane-lined rural rides of the Piedmontese countryside, it is surprising to discover so many feudal landscapes, poised on once importantly strategic hilltops. Of these, the Castello di Agliè is one of the most majestic and magical. On approaching the castle from the south across open fields, a capacious 18th-century water garden can be glimpsed, embraced by symmetrical balustraded ramps which lead to the park beyond. The castle was erected in the 17th century for Count Filippo d'Agliè to the designs of di Castelmonte, but was purchased by the Savoy family in 1764 and improved by Birago di Borgaro.

The first part of the formal gardens comprises a round pool encircled by stately trees, including larch *(Larix decidua)*, cedars *(Cedrus libani* ssp. *atlantica* Glauca Group*)*, beech *(Fagus sylvatica* 'Pendula'*)*, ginkgos, limes, wellingtonia *(Sequoiadendron giganteum)*, and tulip trees; the second area of the gardens is partly confined by walls inset with alcoves and focuses on a scruffy parterre. The highlight is the magnificent walled landscape park. Encompassed by a broad belt of trees, it has an open area with groves of pines, spruce, oak, and hornbeam. A lake with a rusticated stone bridge and a decayed boathouse has a small *cottage orné* on an island.

La Mortola (Giardini Botanici Hanbury)

Location: A 10 Genoa-Ventimiglia, exit Ventimiglia 8km (5 miles); 4km (2½ miles) W of Ventimiglia on SS 1

open: 30 Oct to 30 Mar, daily except Wed, 10am–4pm; 31 Mar to 14 Jun and 30 Sep to 29 Oct, daily, 10am–5pm; 15 Jun to 29 Sep, daily, 9am–6pm. Guided tours by appointment (0184 2295077)

Further information from:
La Mortola, C.so Montecarlo
18030 Latte, loc. La Mortola (IM)
Tel: 0184 229582

Nearby sights of interest:
The old town of Ventimiglia

A visit to this magnificent 40 ha (100 acre) garden, planted by Sir Thomas Hanbury and his botanist brother Daniel from 1867, remains a high spot in any gardener's itinerary. The site, on a steep promontory falling to the sea, is dramatically beautiful and the planting rare and extraordinary, covering an unusually wide range between desert succulents, exotic agaves, aloes, and cycads on the upper slopes, to roses and sages nearer the villa, as well as orchards of citrus fruits. Indigenous plants from the region have been preserved in uncultivated pockets and added to over the years. Rainfall is surprisingly high and often experienced in heavy storms which can sweep away plants and paths.

The original aim at La Mortola – named after the thickets of wild myrtle *(Myrtus communis)* on the rocky shore – was to grow everything that would flourish on the site. Sir Thomas Hanbury's son, Cecil, and his wife, Dorothy, continued the planting programmes but also added more architectural features. Linking steps, paths, fountains, pools, and belvederes unite the whole garden and link the various planting themes.

Flights of steps pause at frequent landings to lead the visitor down a descending cypress avenue, with smaller paths that criss-cross the cliff side to reveal hidden pockets of planting. The succulents are on the highest, sunniest slopes, and exotic trees – tender eucalyptus, Mexican cypress *(Cupressus guadalupensis)*, acacias, melaleucas, and metrosideros, are scattered throughout. A pergola 274m (300yds) long is clothed with red passion flowers, pink begonias, and the scented *Jasminum polyanthum*, and on the bottom slopes orchards are being renewed and the old parterre of lavender and rosemary reinstated.

From 1960 La Mortola was threatened with closure and became neglected. After years of international agitation, the garden's future and renewal of planting is ensured. Now named the Hanbury Botanic Gardens and belonging to the University of Genoa, it has regained its past glory under the leadership of Professor Paola Profumo.

In the Hanbury gardens some more architectural features were added at the beginning of the 20th century.

open: By appointment only (02 76002034), May to Sep

Further information from:
Cardano, 22010 Grandola e Uniti (Co)
Tel: 0344 32120

Nearby sights of interest:
Menaggio; Villa Carlotta, Tremezzo; environs of Lake Como (by boat).

The gardens of the Villa Bagatti Valsecchi are terraced to reveal a panoramic view of Lake Como.

3 *Lake Como: Villa Bagatti Valsecchi*

Location: 40km (25 miles) from Como, on SS 340, at Menaggio take road to Porlezza and Lugano

The villa perches high above Lake Como. The garden has two distinctive parts, and is spread over a series of broad hanging terraces, the largest of which, the "old garden", is adjacent to the villa. The area forms a spacious viewing platform and is laid to lawn and encompassed with gravel paths. A central pool is surrounded by dwarf conifers and Japanese maple. From this terrace there is a staggering panorama of hanging woods and distant peaks, or one can peer over the railings into the dizzying depths of of the gorge beneath.

Access to the "new garden" is gained by passing beneath a lofty stone arcade at the north-east corner of the villa. Several terraces are retained by stone walls connected by stone steps. An imposing ramp, the *scalinata in pietra*, framed by clumps of majestic cypresses, is planted with tufts of alpines. Throughout these gardens serpentine borders are planted with enamelled drifts of annuals and perennials, and the walls are clad with a profusion of trailing and prostrate flowering plants.

---

open: Apr to Oct, Tue, Thu, Sat and Sun, 10am–12.30pm, 3.30pm–6.30pm
open: Groups only by previous appointment

Further information from:
22016 Lenno (CO)
Tel: 0344 56110

Nearby sights of interest:
Villa Carlotta, resorts of Tremezzo and Menaggio.

4 *Lake Como: Villa del Balbianello*

Location: SS 340 from Como "Regina" Lungalago, 27km (16½ miles)

The setting of Villa Balbianello on the Lavedo point, combined with the romantic arrival at the water gates landing stage, turn the expedition into an arcadian delight. Remote from lakeside tourism, exquisite Balbianello, set in sylvan woods of pine, soaring cypress and oak with pollarded plane trees and manicured lawns and flowerbeds, seems enchanted.

With unparalleled views down the three branches of the lake, and fronting the promontory of Serbelloni, the first villa was built in 1540, but was later moved to a new site inland to protect it from flooding. By 1787 the property was acquired by Cardinal Durini, who erected a *casino* with a loggia in 1790, open to the sun and breezes, and today "trellised" with *Ficus pumila* and flanked by a library and music room. Now belonging to FAI, the garden is maintained to an exceptionally high standard and visitors can delight in the beauty and enchantment of the site.

Como: Villa Brivio-Sforza

Location: 20km (12½ miles) from Lecco left branch on the eastern shore of Lake Como. Off the road between Calco and Mercate on SS 36

Situated in the foothills of Mount Brianza, the villa has a splendid view over the gardens and distant plains. Entry is through a north-facing courtyard to a broad terrace, giving on to an 18th-century garden in which shady alleys of hornbeam cut as pillars march out from the edge of the façade and then open to form a rondel enclosing a pool – all echoing and clearly inspired by the layout of Bernini's colonnade at St Peter's in Rome. The central lawns are edged with thick box.

The Renaissance villa was substantially altered and a garden laid out by Muttoni in the early 18th century. The elaborate Italian Garden – its terraces can be seen in Marcantonio dal Re's engravings of 1726 that hang inside the villa – dates to the beginning of the 18th century. Except for the first terrace, with its pavilions of tufa and pebble mosaic, this earlier garden was destroyed in 1837 to make way for an English-style park in which many trees – liquidambars, tulip trees and oaks – have now grown to a large size. The villa was later realigned and its façade rebuilt to its present form, with a new garden of hornbeam arcades before it. Elaborately carved balustrades in the local sandstone – known as *pietra arenaria* – define the edges of the terraces and top the double staircases. Little known today, this garden is one of Italy's most important Baroque layouts.

open: By appointment only

Further information from:
Marchese Annibale Brivio Sforza, Belgiojoso, Merate, 22055 Lecco

Nearby sights of interest:
Environs of Lake Como (by boat).

The remaining terraces of the early 18th-century Italian garden at Villa Brivio-Sforza is dominated by the pavilions of tufa and pebble mosaic.

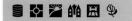

open: Mar and Oct, daily, 9am–11.30am, 2pm–4.30pm; Apr to Sep, daily, 9am–6pm
open: As above

Further information from:
Via Regina 2, 22019 Tremezzo (CO). Tel: 0344 40405 and 41011

Nearby sights of interest:
Tremezzo; Lake Como (by boat).

Formal staircases below the Villa Carlotta back a pool beyond wrought-iron gates.

Lake Como: Villa Carlotta

Location: On the west shore of Lake Como reached from Como by ferry or 30km (18½ miles) by SS 340 "Regina" Lungolago

The elegant 18th-century villa had its own landing place on the lake, with access through tall gates to the base of the terrace. The villa and garden in this ideal setting, although today entered by a side entrance, are no disappointment. Around the house an 18th-century formal layout, with lemon arbours on the terraces, tall camellia hedges and flowerbeds, suit the architecture, while a little further from the villa, plunging into woodland, one discovers a relaxed English-style garden – made after 1843 – filled with interesting trees, shrubs and flowers, a range far beyond the conventional rhododendrons and azaleas which decorate many of these lakeside gardens.

The villa was built in 1745 and later given as a wedding present to Carlotta, Duchess of Saxe-Meiningen who, with her husband, created the landscape garden and began the botanical collection. The original terraces remain but the view is narrowed to fit the façade of the villa, with deep bosky woods and hedges on either side, concealing *giardini segreti*. Imaginative planting on the sunny terraces includes twining climbers, jasmine and roses, and palm trees which look down on the entrance court and pool. In the more natural garden a dell of tree ferns, thriving in the moist atmosphere, more palms, eucalyptus, Japanese maples, cork oaks, giant magnolias, and cactus reveal the microclimatic conditions, with bananas and flowering orchids creating an exotic semi-tropical jungle effect.

open: Guided tours available, 31 Mar to 2 Oct, Sun and public holidays. 9.30am–12pm, 2.30pm–7pm; also open August, daily, 2.30-7pm. Tours for groups of not less than 20 persons can be arranged on other days

Further information from:
Dr Marchesini, Piazza Cicogna 8, 21050 Bisuchio (VA)
Tel and fax: 0332 471134

Nearby sights of interest:
Lake Lugano and Lugano.

Lake Como: Villa Cicogna Mozzoni

Location: 10km (6¼ miles) from Varese on the SS 344

The entrance to the villa gives on to a cool cobbled arcade with bubbling fountains drowning the noise of traffic. It is a fine ensemble of buildings, built into a steep hillside, dating to the 16th century, with magnificent garden rooms on three levels, an arcaded courtyard frescoed by the Campi brothers from Cremona, broad terraces – the upper garden leads directly into the *piano nobile* of the villa – and a spectacular water staircase, flanked with cypresses, descending from a small pavilion to face the windows of the *salone*. Lake Lugano to the north can be glimpsed from the garden adjacent to the northern façade of the house (not usually accessible). The bones of this important garden remain intact with grottoes, fountains and water jokes set along the paths, all still in working order. The gardens and buildings interlock and flow together as a model of architectural ingenuity, creating alternating patterns of sunlight and shadow that add a further dimension to enjoyment.

There was a hunting lodge here in the 15th century belonging to the Mozzoni family. This was transformed into a Renaissance villa of Tuscan style by the scholarly and well travelled Ascanio Mozzoni between 1530 and 1560. Trellis work frescoes of fruit and flowers in the loggia of the Court of Honour by the brothers Campi date to this period. After 1592, Angiola Mozzoni, the last of the line, and her husband, Count Gianpietro Cicogna, further extended and embellished the garden, to create the detail of the courtyard spaces.

The inner courtyard of the 16th-century Villa Cicogna Mozzoni has the original balustraded fishponds, although the parterre planting is more modern.

open: All year, variable hours depending upon season; summer 9am–7pm
open: Only as a conference centre

Further information from:
Via IV Novembre 18, 22050
Varenna (LC)
Tel: 0341 830113
Fax: 0341 830401

Nearby sights of interest:
Villa Monastero; environs of Lake Como (by boat).

8 *Lake Como: Villa Cipressi*

Location: 44km (27 miles) NW of Lecco, take SS 36 direction Colico

Villa Cipressi is magnificently poised upon a steep, rocky promontory into which are carved a series of shallow, winding terraces, ramps and steps which glide gracefully down to the shore of Lake Como.

The first terrace, which has a pool at its centre, commands stunning views over the lake which are framed by the cypress trees which give the villa its name. Beyond a heavily embowered pergola, the terrace leads to two sets of stairs which descend to a pair of lower terraces, which wind around the cliff.

The margins of the terraces are planted with Mediterranean shrubs and vines, interspersed with magnolia, eucalyptus, pittosporum and groupings of lavender and agave. The ramped terraces wind their way gently down to a landing stage, and a watergate framed by giant piers entwined with wisteria. At the north end of the terraces there is a small enclosed garden planted with aspidistra, ivy, palm, and magnolia.

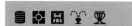

open: To hotel guests; group visits can be arranged; Mar to Nov, free entry at weekends

Further information from:
Cernobbio, Lago di Como
Tel: 031 511471 and 512471

Nearby sights of interest:
Cernobbio; environs of Lake Como.

The axial view between the pavilions at the Villa d'Este.

9 *Lake Como: Villa d'Este*

Location: On the road past Cernobbio, NW of Como, on the lake shore

Built in the 16th century by Pellegrini, the villa is now much altered, although the basic design of the formal garden and water cascade, descending from the Hercules fountain, still remains. Pellegrini's stucco, pebble and marble mosaic hemicycle *nymphaeum* was redecorated in 1894, with bas-reliefs on the themes of solitude and love. Designed as pavilions for entertaining with double steps rising to a oval pool, the Villa d'Este is now the only Renaissance layout on the lake. In the latter part of the 18th century the villa was owned by the Jesuits, but was later purchased by the Marquis Calderara, who added the cypresses which flank the cascade. After his death, his widow built turrets and fortresses on the garden cliffs to amuse her second husband.

Originally called the Villa Garrovo, it was re-named Villa d'Este by Caroline of Brunswick – the estranged wife of the future George IV – who owned the villa for five years from 1815 and had family connections with the d'Este family of Ferrara. The villa was later owned by a celebrated Italian patriot, Baron Ippolito Ciani, as well as by the Empress Fedorovna, mother of Czar Alexander II of Russia, who lived there between 1868–73. After 1873 the new owners decided to convert the villa into a luxury hotel, adding a third storey and widening the façade.

Lake Como: Giardini di Villa Melzi

Location: SS 83 by Bellagio 30km (18½ miles) from Como

open: 23 Mar to 4 Nov, daily. Mar, Oct and Nov 9am–12.30pm, 2pm–6.30pm; Apr to Sep 9am–6.30pm
open: Museum and chapel open as above

Further information from:
22021 Bellagio Loppia (CO)

Nearby sights of interest:
Bellagio; Villa Serbelloni; views of Tremezzo; environs of Lake Como (by boat).

The landscape garden at Villa Melzi on the shore of Lake Como is planted with both native trees and shrubs and many exotics, introduced during the 19th century. The writer Stendhal stayed at the villa just after its completion in 1810 and felt that "Nothing in the world could compare to the charms of these days spent on the Milanese lakes."

The villa was designed in semi-classical style by Albertolli, facing the lakes and supported with balustraded terraces. Pollarded plane trees and some flowerbeds for annuals establish a formal rhythm, but the garden is primarily an English-style pleasure park with outstanding tree specimens. The tender *Pinus montezumae*, giant redwoods (sequoias and sequoiadendrons), tulip trees, white pines *(Pinus strobus)*, red oaks, swamp cypresses from North America, Japanese maples, *Cryptomeria japonica*, camphor trees *(Cinnamoinum camphora)*, and camellias from Asia, the latter planned to give an oriental air to a picturesque pool, all thrive in the mild winters, hot summers and high rainfall of the Larian Lake. The collection of sculpture is eclectic with Egyptian and Roman sarcophagi and busts and statues found under trees and along the walks.

At the Villa Melzi a good collection of exotics frames the view to Lake Como and mountains on the north shore.

open: 1 May to 31 Oct, daily except Tues; tours also available by appointment

open: As above

Further information from:
Via Polvani, 222050 Varenna (LC)
Tel: 0341 830129

Nearby sights of interest:
Varenna; Villa Cipressi; environs of Lake Como (by boat).

A view of the Villa Monastero from Lake Como shows the waterfront loggia and gives a hint of the luxuriant Mediterranean and exotic tropical planting.

Lake Como: Villa Monastero

Location: 44km (27 miles) NW of Lecco, take SS 36 direction Colico

Villa Monastero, situated at the junction of Lakes Lecco and Como, has its origins in the early 13th century when it was built as a Cistercian convent dedicated to St Mary Magdalene. When the order was suppressed in the mid 16th century the building was converted to a residential villa; and we are informed that in 1569 Lelio Mornico di Cortenova "spared no effort to make his father's house even more beautiful", and, as the story goes, "he turned the Lake into a garden". For many years the villa bore the name Leliana in recognition of the man who transformed it. After several changes of owner, the villa was sold in 1899 to the Austrian Walter Kress, who introduced many of the exotic plants which we see today, such as the palms and agaves. The Kresses made numerous improvements to the villa, building the waterfront loggia and the decorative balustrades, and erecting the wellhead and the Moorish coffee-house. Since the early 20th

century the garden has been renowned for its array of luxuriant Mediterranean and tropical vegetation, as well as its fountains, pavilions, statuary, and other garden ornamentation. Among the outstanding plants to be found in the garden are palms, eucalyptus, tangerines, grapefruits, camphor, and *Magnolia grandiflora*. In the *parco* there are collections of roses and cinerarias. Stunning views of the villa are gained from Lake Como or from the terraces of the neighbouring Villa Cipressi (p.22). The visitor is recommended to approach the villa from the south, taking the narrow road which snakes up the shore of Lake Lecco from Mandello. The road from Lecco, with its remarkable perforated tunnels, provides tantalizing views over Lake Lecco. Since 1953 Villa Monastero has been, like the neighbouring Villa i Cipressi, an international conference centre.

12 *Lake Como: Villa Pizzo*

Location: On west shore of Lake Como, 8km (5 miles) from Como, just past Cernobbio. on N 340 "Regina" Lungolago

open: Apr to Oct by appointment and Mon 10am–5pm

Further information from:
Tel: 031 511700 Gabrielli Togliani
Fax: 02 48708331 Raimondo Sannina

Nearby sights of interest:
Resort of Cernobbio; environs of Lake Como (by boat).

The villa lies on the west shore of Lake Como below the road to Menaggio. It is a glorious garden site that opens out to reveal views up and down the lake and closes again to cool shady walks. *Trachelospermum jasminoides* clothes high walls, camphor trees and tea olive *(Osmanthus fragrans)*, Californian bay rum *(Umbellularia californica)* and, under the house façade, lemon-scented verbenas *(Aloysia triphylla)* mix exotic fragrance with the familiar Mediterranean aroma of bay, cypress, box and myrtle. Figs and specimen *Buxus balearica* grow on the shore. Huge evergreen magnolias *(Magnolia grandiflora)*, loquats *(Eriobotrya japonica)*, a weeping *Sophora japonica*, *Albizia julibrissin*, ginkgos, Kentucky coffee trees *(Gymnocladus dioica)* and pruned crape myrtles *(Lagerstroemia indica)*, groves of bamboos and tall koelreuterias are other introductions.

At Villa Pizzo scented *Trachelospermum jasminoides* trail over an arbour.

    Acquired by the Austrian Viceroy, Archduke Rainieri, in 1842, much of the landscape-style planting originates with his head gardener, Ettore Villoresi. The drive is flanked by pollarded plane trees and clouds of Banksian roses falling to the lower terraces, where roses and honeysuckle grow on an arbour. A yellow-flowered *Caesalpinia* from Japan hangs over the water. Around the house a formal Italian garden has been "anglicized" with blue ceanothus, lespedeza, lantanas, and charming, pale pink geraniums.

Lake Como: Villa Serbelloni

open: 15 Apr to 15 Oct, daily, except Mon; guided visits only at 11am and 4pm booked ahead (A.P.T. tel: 031 950204; fax: 951551)

open: Functions as an international study centre run by the Rockefeller Foundation

Further information from:
Via Garibaldi, 22021 Bellagio (CO)
Tel: 031 950105

Nearby sights of interest:
Resort of Bellagio; Villa Melzi; environs of Lake Como (by boat).

Location: SS 583 from Como to Bellagio 30km (18½ miles) or by boat from Como, Tramezzo or Varenna

The promontory of Serbelloni, originally a barren rock above the lake shore at Bellagio and once possibly the site of Pliny the Younger's villa "Tragedia", later became a medieval fortress. From its highest point, well worth the ascent and now clothed with luxurious woods, there are breathtaking views down all three arms of Lake Como and to the surrounding mountains.

The villa itself was built after 1539 for Count Francesco Sfrondati. The original garden had fine orange and citrus trees, figs, olives, and laurels; it was Sfrondati who planted the hill above with orchards and native woodland. The property passed to Duke Alessandro Serbelloni in 1788 and he created the grand Italian-style terraces around the villa which we see today, now clothed with excellent planting of santolinas, phlomis and other natives, mixed with drought-tolerant plants from other countries. Statues, busts, grottoes, and curiosities of archeological digs are all part of the garden scene.

In 1825 the writer Stendhal recorded his impressions: " higher up, the sacred wood of the Sfrondato and the bold promontory, separating the two arms of the lake...so luxuriantly beautiful...a sublime and enchanting spectacle, which the most renowned

The view from the medieval fortress at the highest point on Serbelloni reveals all branches of the lake.

sight in the world...does not surpass". The garden was restored in 1842, and further improved in recent years by Ella Walker, the Principessa della Torre e Tasso, who in 1959 gave the property to the Rockefeller Foundation as an international study centre.

The woods, with hornbeam, hazel and holly, and carpets of Solomon's seal, lily of the valley, hepaticas, and hellebores, between sheets of butcher's broom, are enchanting.

Lake Como: Villa Sommi-Picenardi

Location: 15km (9½ miles) SW of Lecco. SS 36 to Calco, then SS 342 direction Como

open: Apr to Oct by appointment only

Further information from:
Viale Sommi Picenardi 8, 22056
Olgiate Molgora (LC)
Tel: 039 508333
Fax: 039 9910415

Nearby sights of interest:
Environs of Lake Como (by boat).

Great trees, in an English-style 19th-century park, greet the visitor at the front of the 18th-century villa, leaving the contemporary formal garden to come as a delightful surprise. The terraced layout of double staircases and ramps, ornamented with coloured mosaic pebbles, statues on balustrades, carved stone swags, and fountains in niches, all backed by a screen of tall cypresses, must have been planned to be viewed from the windows of the *piano nobile* as if it was a stage set. Pools and fountains were added in the 19th century on the flat space between the villa and the terraces. A magnificent oriental plane tree *(Platanus orientalis)* and a fern-leaved beech *(Fagus sylvatica* 'Asplenifolia'*)* shelter the south side of the house.

At Sommi-Picenardi the formal terraced garden behind the villa dates to the early 18th century.

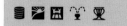

Villa Durazzo Pallavicini

Location: 15km (9¼ miles) from Genoa by A 10

open: All year, daily except Mon; winter 10am–5pm; summer 9am–7pm

Further information from:
Via Ignazio Pallavicini, 16155 Pegli, Genova; Commune of Genova
Tel: 010 6982865

Nearby sights of interest:
City of Genoa; Museo Navale at Pegli.

The Temple of Diana at the Villa Durazzo Pallavicini is one of the many architectural features in this romantic 19th-century park.

The Durazzo Pallavicini is a remarkable park in eclectic style. It was created by Marquis Ignazio Alessandro Pallavicini between 1840–46 in the grounds of a villa inherited from his aunt, who had, in 1794, planted a small botanical garden. Ignazio appointed Michele Canzio, the art director of the theatre Carlo Felice at Genoa, as the curator. The plan of the park is comparable to a drama in many acts, to represent the detachment of man from the cares of life in order to return to nature. Various features recall the main civilizations of the world. The visitor is stimulated by continous changing of scenes, merging with an abundance of flourishing vegetation.

The visit begins at the Gothic Temple and continues along a straight path leading to the Kaffehaus and the Triumphal Arch, then a passage from the classic world to a wilder one, with the Hermitage, the Old Lake and the Spring. The walk proceeds through a Mediterranean Garden, with many palm trees, to the Castle of the Captain of the Park, a folly in medieval style and to a grotto, symbol of Hades. From the darkness of the grotto the visitor reaches a lake where, by contrast, the dazzling sunlight gives the impression of being in heaven. By the lake the Temple of Diana, symbolic of the ancient classical world, is surrounded by four Tritons emerging from the water. The lake is further decorated with more follies: a Chinese Bridge and Pagoda, and a Turkish Kiosk, from which there is a splendid view of the park. On the south side of the meandering lake the Temple of Flora, a small pavilion on the edge of a secret flower garden, is provided with a small conservatory, ornamented with flowers in pots, and has a pier for boats, once used for excursions on the lake.

The park has many remarkable plants, such as the tropical camphor tree, *Cinnamomum camphora*, and a Lebanon cedar *(Cedrus libani)* by the lake, besides many palm trees, such as the desert fan palm, *Washingtonia filifera*, and the thread palm, *Washingtonia robusta*, both from southwest North America, in the Mediterranean Garden.

Parco Villa Grimaldi, "Il Roseto di Nervi"

Location: 14km (8½ miles) from Genoa in direction of Levante

The Roseto or Rose Garden of the Villa Grimaldi Fassio is one of
three extensive former villa gardens acquired by the Commune
in the early 20th century to form a 9ha (22 acre) park on the
seaside at Nervi. The grounds of the Villa Gropallo, Villa Serra
and Villa Grimaldi still, however, retain their individual identity.
The Parco Grimaldi is the easternmost of the three gardens.
Here the roses are either trained over pergolas, or planted on
pillars or as single specimens of groups in beds. While many
of the roses are winners of "Premio Genova" of the Concorso
Internazionale della Rosa Rifiorente, the floral selection and
display lacks the sparkle of many English rose gardens.
Nevertheless, the gentle climate allows a backdrop of subtropical
plants to contrast with the roses. There are orange-blossom
scented hedges of *Pittosporum tobira*, walls clad with bougainvillea
(Bougainvillea spectabilis), thread palm *(Washingtonia robusta)*,
stone pines, and cycads. The gardens of the neighbouring villas
are laid out *all'inglese* and display a distinguished array of trees
and shrubs, including bunya bunya *(Araucaria bidwillii)*, cork
oaks *(Quercus suber)*, and Monterey cypress *(Cupressus macrocarpa)*.

open: Daily, dawn to dusk

Further information from:
Via Capolungo 9, 16167
Genoa-Nervi
Tel: 010 3773475

Nearby sights of interest:
Town of Nervi; city of Genoa.

In the Rose Garden in the Parco
Villa Grimaldi many other plants,
including exotics enjoying the
mild climate, add to the
botanical interest.

Lake Maggiore: Isola Bella

Location: On Lago di Maggiore opposite Lido di Stresa, reached from Arona, Stresa, Baveno, Pallanza, Laveno by boat

First seen from the shore at Stresa, the palace and gardens of Isola Bella seem to float on the lake's surface like a great ship of state, its prow the theatrical ten-terraced garden, with statues silhouetted on the marble balustrades. Isola Bella is undoubtedly one of the most dramatic 17th-century Baroque gardens in Italy, romanticized over three centuries by the profusion of its flower-laden hanging gardens. A visit promises gratification to the architectural and garden historian as well as to the keen gardener, who finds the rare and tender plants a stimulating experience.

Originally a barren island, the vast Baroque palace and its garden was begun for Count Carlo Borromeo in 1632. Building continued until 1671 under his sons Conte Vitaliani and his

The formal parterres below the terrace and water theatre are planted with annuals.

One of the pavilions containing pumping equipment to get water into the vast storage tank below the stone terrace.

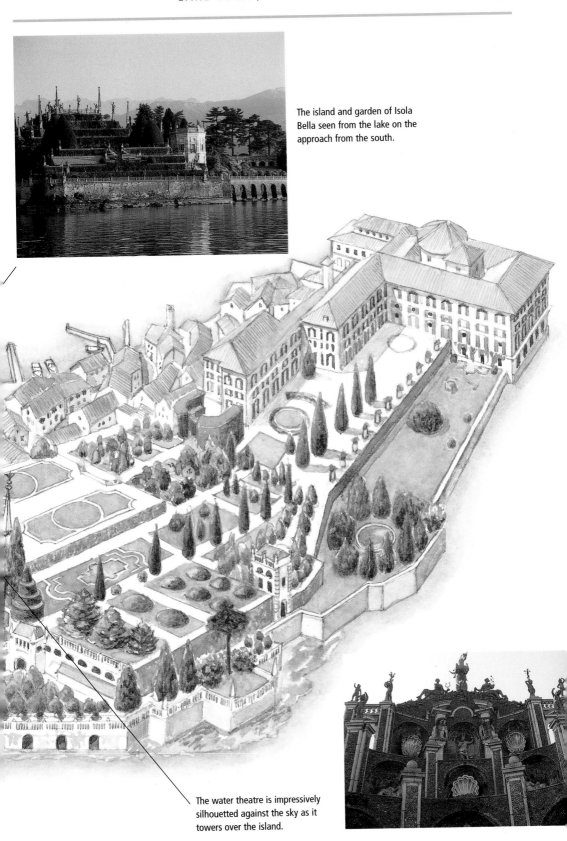

The island and garden of Isola Bella seen from the lake on the approach from the south.

The water theatre is impressively silhouetted against the sky as it towers over the island.

brother Gilberto, who employed the architects Fontana and Castelli, together with a host of other artists and sculptors. With earth imported from the shores of the lake the main structure of the garden layout was completed by the 1690s, although the original plans of the palace, especially its northern façade, were abandoned until quite recently when work once more resumed. The island, together with the neighbouring Isola Madre (p.34), still belongs to Prince Borromeo-Arese.

The six subterranean grottoes through which the garden is reached are sumptuously embellished with delicately tinted stucco, pebble mosaic and shellwork, providing a cool prelude before the visitor emerges into the summer glare. A model of the palace and garden in one of the rooms on the first floor, showing the irregular form of the island and how the garden is not on an axis with the main buildings, is useful for orientation. One of the first descriptions of Isola Bella comes from the English diarist Bishop Gilbert Burnet, who visited in 1685 and found the situation "one of the loveliest spots of ground in the World". A print by Marc Antonio dal Re, published in 1726, shows the island, palace and terraces from the south east when architectural features were still uncluttered with plant shapes and foliage. In 1797 banquets and concerts were held in the garden to honour Napoleon and Josephine and their entourage, after the French victory at the battle of Marengo.

Stairs up to the great water theatre are edged with pots planted with box. The unicorn, symbol of the Borromeo family, dominates the view looking down over the five high terraces.

The visitor emerges into the gently curving, shaded Courtyard of Diana, from which steps ascend to the central axis of the garden stretching south at an angle to the palace. To the left of the courtyard is the Theatre of Hercules, with a central niche in the semi-circular wall containing a statue of Hercules complete with club and lion skin. Above lie the original grass parterres, now overflowing and shaded with exotic evergreen trees and shrubs. Two large camphor trees *(Cinnamomium camphora)*, flank the gates, with magnolias, camellias, pittosporums, *Myrtus apiculata* from Chile, and native Mediterranean myrtle, all shaded by tall tulip trees. The central space is dominated by the Water Theatre, topped by the prancing statue of a unicorn – symbol of the Borromeo family – a vast façade of five terraces rising 37m (121ft) above the surface of the lake. *Putti* on the pebble-encrusted pillars, gods and goddesses, and scallop shell fountains and water-jokes (designed by Carlo Fontana) in the niches, and allegories of the triumphs of the Borromeo family, all add a charming fantasy to the whole conception, the architectural details only softened by box balls arrayed in pots on the steps on either side, and flag irises and royal ferns by the pool. Two reclining figures represent the rivers Tosa and Ticino, which feed the lake.

Concealed behind the theatrical façade is a broad stone terrace, the "poop" of the ship, which hides a vast cistern to which water is pumped from the lake. The steep terraces, planted with espaliered fruit and roses, descend in pyramidal shape to reach a French-style Baroque box parterre and lemon trees in decorative pots on the fifth terrace. Finials, statues and wrought iron flowers in stone vases define the spaces, soaring skywards in fantastic splendour. Two hexagonal towers stand near the shore framing the terraces from the south; one is a summerhouse, the other houses the pumping equipment for the reservoir. On the eastern side of the island there is an aviary and more fine trees, while to the sheltered west orange trees are espaliered against the lower terrace walls, and a walk of pomegranates is underplanted with lily of the valley. An old specimen cork oak (*Quercus suber*) grows almost on the lake shore. Many of the walls are tightly covered with the creeping fig, *Ficus pumila*. Under the present management new and interesting planting continues to extend the range of plants and everything is excellently maintained. The exit is through the west side of the fifth terrace.

The Courtyard of Diana is so called after a statue of the goddess that stands in the central niche of the courtyard.

The formal parterres on the south side of the island, viewed from the stone terrace behind the Water Theatre.

open: 27 Mar to 24 Oct,
daily, 9am–12pm, 1.30pm–5.30pm
(Oct 9.30am–12.30pm,
1.30pm–5pm)
open: Guided tours available

Further information from:
Isola Madre (VB)
Tel: 0323 31261

Nearby sights of interest:
The Borromean Islands, including
Isola Bella; Arona, Baveno,
Pallanza, Stresa, including the Villa
Pallvicino; environs of Lake
Maggiore (by boat).

18 *Lake Maggiore: Isola Madre*

Location: Reached from Stresa, Pallanza, Baveno, Laveno, Arona by boat

On Isola Madre the semi-tropical planting provides a lush paradise, enhanced by groups of white peacocks. The original garden was planted around the unfinished Renaissance villa with formal terracing providing shelter for citrus and orchards. In the early 19th century Prince Gilberto replaced the orchards with ornamental trees and shrubs, including a fine swamp cypress *(Taxodium distichum)*. In 1850 Conte Vitaliani planted recently introduced trees and shrubs, such as palm trees, on the terraces.

Citrus fruits still flourish, accompanied by crape myrtle, hibiscus, leptospermum and acacias. In sheltered spots, bouganvillea, agaves and the rare *Nolina longifolia* take advantage of the microclimate with groups of *Beschorneria yuccoides*.

The landscape woods have groves of native trees – aromatic cypress, bay and pine – interplanted with camphor *(Cinnamomum camphora)*, pepper trees *(Schinus molle)* and styrax. Pathways are lined with magnolias, camellias, rhododendrons, and azaleas, while a walk of clipped bay strikes a more formal note framing a north-facing watergate. A specimen Kashmir cypress *(Cupressus torulosa* 'Cashmeriana' syn. *C. cashmeriana)* is an important feature.

On Isola Madre the planting
takes advantage of the
microclimatic situation and
arbours create patterns of
light and shade.

Lake Maggiore: Villa della Porta Bozzolo

Location: 22km (13½ miles) from Varese SS 394 direction Laveno, after Gemonio right turn to Valcuvia

Few sites in Lombardy have such a dramatic impact on the eye as the gardens of Villa della Porta Bozzolo. A long approach past parterres to steps, enclosed by balustraded terraces, leads the eye upwards to an octagonal clearing ringed by cypresses, terminating in a central fountain, the vista then stretching up an almost vertical slope, a ride cut through the forest trees and reaching to the horizon. It is a classic example of the dramatic use of natural topography to create architectural effect. The garden was made in the late 17th century and the 16th-century villa was left to one side of the axis so as not to interfere with the perspective.

It was decided to shift the central axis of the garden to be at right angles with the house. The result, rare in Lombardy, resembles the Roman villas of the 16th century, but the detail of the curving Baroque walls, framing gateways and niches, and the extended view, have a distinct French nuance. A cross axis from the main doors of the villa leads along an avenue of deciduous oaks to a temple dedicated to Apollo and the Muses.

The balustrading and terraces with pebble-patterned paths have been carefully restored; fountains play at each level and *putti* stand guardian on the balustrades. The simple planting of pink roses, replacing lemons in pots, is attractive if not authentic.

open: Oct to Dec daily 10.am-5pm, Feb to Sept, Daily 10am-6pm. Closed Mons, the last two weeks in Dec and in Jan

open: (With frescoes of the school of Magatti from Varese) As above but closed daily 1-2pm; guided tours by appointment

Further information from:
Via le Bozzolo
21030 Casalzuigno (VA)
Tel: 0332 624136
For more information FAI Milano
Office tel: 02 4815556

Nearby sights of interest:
Giardini Estensi in Varese;
environs of Lake Maggiore
(by boat).

At the magnificent Villa della Porta Bozzolo the main axis reaches through the garden to an octagonal meadow and carries the eye up the slope between flanking cypresses.

■ ⦿

open: 16 Mar–31 Oct, daily, 9am–6pm

Further information from:
Via Nazionale del Sempione Sud
28049 Stresa (VB)
Tel: 0323 30556

Nearby sights of interest:
Zoo in park; resort of Stresa; Lake Maggiore (by boat).

Roses and *Trachelospermum* in the formal garden at Pallavicino.

20 *Lake Maggiore: Parco Villa Pallavicino*

Location: 16km (10 miles) from Verbania; take the SS 33 to Feriolo and then the SS 34 or the A 26 and exit Brovello-Carpugnino

Situated above Lake Maggiore with panoramic views, this well maintained park – also a zoological garden – has a magnificent collection of exotic trees. There are also the relics of a formal garden and greenhouses, where scented *Trachelospermum jasminoides* frame massed rose beds and wide beds of annuals. In the 19th century the existing planting was enriched by the Duke of Vallombrosa, who laid out the park in naturalistic style. Since 1862 the villa and park have been owned by the Pallavicino family.

Giant tulip trees (*Liriodendron tulipifera*), in flower in May, swamp cypresses *(Taxodium distichum)*, liquidambars, and redwoods, are planted in groves with oriental planes and ginkgos, Atlantic and lebanon cedars, horse chestnuts, copper and weeping beech, as well as flowering dogwoods (*Cornus kousa*), an array of magnolias, hedges of camellias, a spreading *Albizia julibrissin*, callistemons, fragrant *Pittosporum tobira*, and Japanese maples. Hostas and goat's beard (*Aruncus dioicus*) grow in shade with ruscus – both *Ruscus aculeatus* and *R. hypoglossum* – with Mexican erigerons seeding in more open rockwalls.

---

open: Guided tours by appointment only on working days during spring, summer and autumn. Contact the Ufficio Cultura Commune di Verbania, Dottoressa Martini (0323 401510)

Further information from:
V. San Remigio 19, 28048
Pallanza-Verbania (VB)
Tel: 0323 504401

Nearby sights of interest:
Resort of Pallanza, including Villa Taranto; Stresa, including Villa Pallavicino; Mt Mottarone; environs of Lake Maggiore (by boat).

21 *Lake Maggiore: Villa San Remigio*

Location: SS 33 along the lake to Feriolo, then SS 34

This garden, laid out at the start of the 20th century, has features derived from earlier classical gardens, besides spectacular views over Lake Maggiore. It is partly a romantic Victorian park and partly an Edwardian interpretation of a Renaissance garden. A visit is fascinating, if only to "discover" the 18th-century statues.

The six terraces below the west face of the villa, with the view of the lake and Mount Mottarone as a backdrop, are linked to the house with grand balustraded steps: niches are decorated with pebble mosaics and dolphins and shell seats. The second terrace is also the ceiling of the enclosed winter garden below, with stream and vaulted grotto, a site for ferns, orchids and sub-tropical plants. Behind the villa the steeply terraced hill descends to a semi-circular wall with niches for statues, possibly inspired by the *nymphaeum* at Villa Aldobrandini.

Lake Maggiore: Villa Taranto-Ente Giardini Botanⁱci

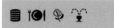

open: 1 Apr–31 Oct, daily, 8.30am–6.30pm

Location: SS 33   g the lake to Feriolo, then SS 34

Further information from:
Via V.Veneto 111, 28048
Pallanza-Verbania (VB)
Tel and fax: 0323 556667

Nearby sights of interest:
Resort of Pallanza; the Borromean Islands, including Isola Bella and Isola Madre; environs of Lake Maggiore (by boat).

The gardens at the Villa Taranto are a mixture of successful naturalistic planting with beautiful and exciting plant species, combined with less immediately attractive formal layouts. For the gardener the garden, with its mild winter climate, high rainfall and hot summers, provides a botanical feast that cannot be missed. It is an eclectic collection; a curving pergola is draped with wisteria and roses, a rare caesalpinia curtains a bridge, and tender shrubs such as gardenias thrive, with great magnolias and sweeps of hostas spreading in the steep-sided valleys.

Trees, shrubs and rhododendrons were the first favourites of the Scotsman Neil McEarchern, who began the garden in 1931. He gave it to the Italian state in 1951. The 18ha (44 acre) gardens were designed to establish a botanical collection taking advantage of the favourable microclimate. McEarchern's success lies in the extraordinary range of species which he acquired, in order to take full advantage of the ideal growing conditions. The rare *Emmenopterys henryi* flowered here in the 1970s.

Henry Cocker, who was trained at Kew, established the extensive collection of herbaceous plants and bulbs. Naturalistic planting in the steep-sided valley is most successful where trees, shrubs and groundcover have matured in graceful sweeps. Elsewhere, although always interesting, planting tends to have elements of a display garden, with less attention paid to associations than to extending the range of specimens, and with gaudy annuals, impeccably maintained, taking the place of perennial plants. In the formal garden, where a central water channel falls over musical chimes, seasonal bedding that includes tulips and pansies in spring and begonias and cannas in summer creates a somewhat municipal atmosphere. The gardens, however, remain a magnificent achievement.

The Villa Taranto has a fine collection of plants, established in the 1930s by the Scot Neil McEarchern.

open: Daily, 9am to dusk

Further information from:
Arenzano (GE)

Nearby sights of interest:
The port, churches and palaces of
the city of Genoa.

The romantic Parco Villa
Negrotto was created towards
the end of the 19th century with
an eclectic choice of buildings
and a fine collection of plants.

23 *Villa Negrotto Cambiaso Pallavicino*

Location: Centre of Arenzano; 15km (9¼ miles) NW of Genoa

The Villa Negrotto Cambiaso Pallavicino, which hovers above the centre of the coastal town of Arenzano, is among the better preserved and more diverse of the large villa gardens characteristic of the Italian Riviera. The villa sits on a densely planted hillside and is surrounded by a landscape park. The present garden is, however, a fragment of a much larger agricultural estate, acquired in 1558 by the Marquese Tobia Pallavicino as a site for a summer residence. Although the estate went through many changes during the early 19th century, the grounds assumed their present layout in the 1880s when the Marchese Luisa Sauli Pallavicino began her improvements – the most significant of which was enclosing the present park. The villa was rendered more picturesque with the additions of crenellations and a lofty tower, and the gardens transformed into a stage set with the building of new stone walls and garden buildings, involving an extensive programme of earth moving and hydraulics to make cascades, grottoes and pools.

Among garden buildings erected at this time were a Swiss chalet – now gone, a shrine, the Cappeletta della Madonna, and an entire medieval village. It was also an express wish of the owner to create a garden of notable botanical diversity and the garden still possesses a variety of interesting plants. They include medake *(Pleioblastus simonii)*, *Bougainvillea spectabilis*, camphor trees *(Cinnamomum camphora)*, *Cryptomeria japonica*, citron *(Citrus medica)*, crape myrtle *(Lagerstroemia indica)*, many palms, including the Mexican fan palm *(Bruhea armata)*, incense cedars *(Calocedrus decurrens)*, and Aleppo pine *(Pinus halepensis)*. The large and elegant 19th-century greenhouse has been recently restored and is soon to be replanted.

24 *Villa Reale*

Location: Monza; 15 km (9¼ miles) N of Milan, Valassina road from Milan to Lecco

The Villa Reale forms an impressive terminus to an immensely long and broad boulevard in Monza, lined with large 19th-century summer residences of the Milanese upper crust. The neo-classical summer palace was built by Empress Maria Theresa of Austria for her son Archduke Ferdinand. At the end of the 18th century the estate went into decline, only to be recast in the English landscape taste in 1803 by the architect and landscape gardener Luigi Canonica. Whilst the public front of the villa remained essentially formal in layout, the landscape beyond the garden front was laid to sweeping lawns interspersed with groups of trees and shrubs. The park was later expanded to its present size by Napoleon Bonaparte. The majestic trees that grace the park include *Quercus palustris, Robinia pseudoacacia, Cedrus deodara, Picea abies, Sequioa sempervirens,* yew, and hornbeams, and there are also impressive stands of beech, ash and spruce. Scattered throughout the *parco* are dozens of neo-Gothic follies, fake battlements, towers, villas, mills, bridges, farmhouses and churches, built between 1805–13 during the residence of Eugène Beauharnais, the adopted son of Napoleon. Among the most charming of these brightly coloured, and almost entirely newly restored *arredi* are the Tempietto Dorico, the Padiglione Carriga, the Torretta Viscontea, and the Mulino del Cantone.

open: Daily, dawn to dusk, free guided tours for organized groups and students by appointment
open: By appointment only

Further information from:
V. le Regina Margherita, 2
20052 Monza (MI)
Tel: 039 2301333 and 365234 for Gruppo Botanico de Monza e Brianza
Tel: 039 366381 for palace, 039 272023269 for King Umberto's apartments and 039 360367 for Villa Mirabello

Nearby sights of interest:
The cathedral in Monza; the city of Milan; the Brianza; environs of Lake Como (by boat).

Although the garden in front of the Villa Reale is formal, the landscape behind the villa was laid out as an English park in Napoleon's time.

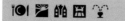

25 *Parco Serra di Comago*

Location: 8km (5 miles) from centre of Genoa, Motorway A 7 direction Genoa-Milano, exit Genoa-Blozaneto, follow road towards Sant'Olcese and villa signs

open: All year, Mar and Oct 9am–5pm, Apr–May 9am–7pm, Jun to Sep 9am–9pm; guided tours available (010 6982776)

Further information from:
Via Carlo Levi, 1, 16010 Sant'Olcese, Genova

Nearby sights of interest:
The port, churches and palaces of the city of Genoa.

The recently restored park was created from about 1850 by the Marquese Carlo Cusani, who transformed a quite large agricultural property into an English landscape park. The English influence is recognizable in the Palazzina Gotica (Gothic Pavilion), built in the style of a Tudor manor house and screening the 18th-century Villa Serra Pinelli, that was "copied" from an illustration in J.C. Loudon's *Encyclopedia of Cottage, Farm and Villa Architecture* (1846). The park is laid out with glades and woody areas, a *palazzina*, a crenellated tower and rustic huts. In the upper area of the large lake water flows in a runnel from a smaller lake, bringing it towards the Gothic Pavilion, crossing the paths and interrupting a visitor's walk with a pleasant sound. A large number of exotic trees include *Liriodendron tulipifera*, *Liquidambar styraciflua*, redwoods and, along the runnel, some specimens of *Taxodium distichum*. Native trees such as *Quercus cerris*, *Carpinus betulus* and *Tilia europaea* are planted in the area near the rustic huts.

26 *Villa Sorra*

Location: 13km (8 miles) SE of Modena, via S9

open: Apr to Sep (Sat 2pm–7pm, Sun 10am–7pm)
open: As above

Further information from:
Gaggio in Piano, Castelfranco Emilia, Modena

Nearby sights of interest:
Cities of Modena and Bologna.

At Villa Sorra the garden still retains some of its original layout.

The garden of Villa Sorra was created from 1827 by the botanist Giovanni Brignoli for the Marchesa Ippolita Sorra as an English landscape park, partly transforming the previous late 17th-century formal garden. It is possible to approach the north front of the villa along two large avenues framed with Lombardy poplars, leading to a large circular space, the *cavallerizza*, that was used for horse races. In spite of informal planting of magnolias and shrubs, the geometry of the 17th-century compartments is still recognizable on the large lawns on both sides of a path leading from the house to woodland, while a gothic tower that belongs to a folly catches the eye. The 17th-century pond and island were transformed into a large moated garden. Small canals, crossed by brickwork bridges, a lake, with islands and peninsulas recall a lagunar landscape. Waterlilies, the yellow *Nuphar lutea* and flag iris *(Iris pseudacorus)* provide interest in the moat. Next to the lake good specimens of bald cypress *(Taxodium distichum)* are interplanted with *Populus alba*, *P. nigra* and oaks. The folly sits on a hill above the lake shore. Resembling a medieval castle, with crenellated walls, a drawbridge and a gothic tower, it commands a view to the Po Valley and the Apennines.

Stupinigi: Palazzina di Caccia

Location: 10km (6¼ miles) SW from Turin; take SS 23 for Pinerolo

The *palazzina* of Stupinigi is a masterpiece by the architect Filippo Juvarra. Built in 1729–34, it has a complex architectural structure, long wings radiating on both sides of the octagonal building. The French architects Bernard, father and son, designed the grounds from 1740. They further interpreted Juvarra's conception by establishing a pattern of radiating roads leading out from the building to penetrate the landscape. The road from Turin leads into the courtyard, ornamented with box-edged parterres. The circular road enclosing the park makes it possible to admire the building, evoking the spirit of movement typical of the Baroque architectural style. A broad avenue on the road from Turin offers an outstanding view of the rear façade and then continues on the south side, effectively bisecting the park. Some irregular paths and a lake provide picturesque nuances, but do not diminish the unity between the palace and the grounds. A visit to the *palazzina* for the Rococo decorations must be included.

open: All year, daily except Mon, winter 9am–12.30pm, 2pm–5pm; summer 9.30am–12.30pm, 2pm–6pm; guided tours by appointment
open: As above

Further information from:
Piazza Principe Amedo 7, 10040 Stupinigi (TO)
Tel: 011 3581220

Nearby sights of interest:
City of Turin, including the cathedral, the churches and palaces.

The great palace of Stupinigi is surrounded by simple box-hedge parterres, bisected by radiating avenues.

Key to gardens

1 Villa Allegri Arvedi
2 Villa Barbarigo Pizzoni Ardemani
3 Castello del Catajao
4 Villa Emo
5 Villa Bettoni
6 Giardino Hruska Botanico
7 Villa Manin

8 University of Padua Botanic Garden
9 Villa Pisani
10 Villa Rizzardi
11 Castello di Miramare
12 Villa Trissino Marzotto
13 Giardino Giusti

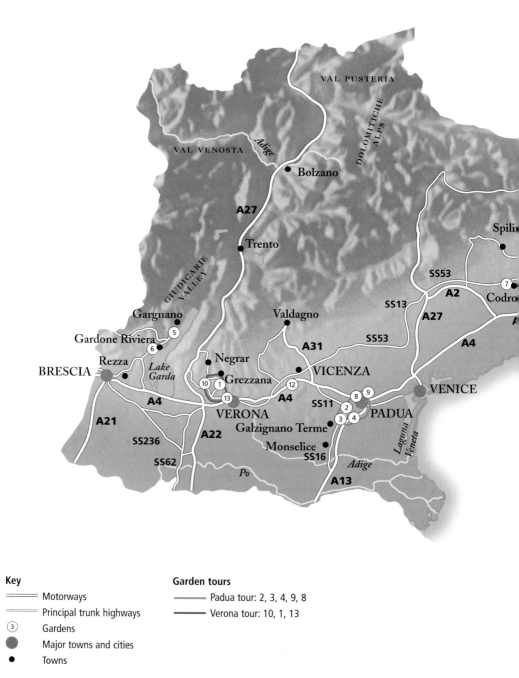

Key

══ Motorways
══ Principal trunk highways
③ Gardens
● Major towns and cities
● Towns

Garden tours

━━ Padua tour: 2, 3, 4, 9, 8
━━ Verona tour: 10, 1, 13

Lake Garda, the Veneto & the North East

Gardens around the sheltered shores of Lake Garda reflect the moderate climate and summer heat but, in the main, the Veneto and Friuli are swept by cold north winds from the Alps. Few of the elegant 16th-century Palladian villas had elaborate gardens, although Palladio carefully related each villa to its site, each façade incorporating fine views to the Alps, the Euganean hills, or the Brenta Valley. The villas were centres of large agricultural estates with *barchesse* for storing grain, serving as summer houses for patrician families from Venice, with the crops being grown almost under the walls of the villas. At the Villa Capra outside Vicenza the countryside sweeps up to the symmetrically arranged steps and porticoes, while at the Villa Emo at Fanzola cornfields frame the façades, linking the "working" estate with the great building and the patrician family with the land. The main exception is the Villa Barbaro at Maser, which had a symmetrical garden

A hornbeam arbour and seat terminate a view at Villa Emo near Monselice.

43

designed for Daniele Barbaro and still shows the remains of parterres. A 17th-century *nymphaeum* and grotto behind the villa are enriched by stucco decoration. Both the Villa Brenzone (no longer open to the public) and the Giardino Giusti in Verona (p.57) date from the 16th century. Villa Brenzone on Lake Garda was designed by the Veronese architect Sanmichele in the early 16th century, and still retains its original layout, with a grove of cypresses sheltering busts of Roman emperors. At Giusti many of the orginal features remain, while the 17th- and 18th-century layouts to be found in such gardens as Villa Rizzardi (p.54) and Villa Allegri Arvedi (p.46), Pisana at Strà (p.53), and the great Manin in Friuli (p.51), reflect French Baroque influence. Villa Barbarigo at Valsanzibio (p.47), recently admirably restored, is a unique late 17th-century garden, planned on two axes with hedged alleys, water canals, a maze, and tall cypresses, laid out in the valley below the villa, backed by the Euganean Hills.

The Padua Botanic Garden (pp.52–53) has great historical importance, sharing with Pisa the distinction of being the oldest in Europe – it was established in 1545. Its circular layout of order beds is perfectly maintained and many trees and shrubs growing in the garden were the first specimens to be grown in Europe after their introduction. Many of these early botanic gardens sacrificed aesthetic appeal by cultivating medicinal herbs for study in square and/or rectangular beds that made for easier genera and species identification. In the Friuli north of Venice many Austrian estates have become landscape parks or had their gardens designed as *giardini inglese* during the 19th century. At Miramare in Trieste (p.55) the Archduke Maximilian planted shelter belts in the 19th century to create micro-climatic conditions so that he could grow exotics.

At the Villa Pisana, Strà, many statues dating from its creation in the 18th century still remain in the French-style woods.

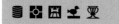

Villa Allegri Arvedi

Location: 10km (6¼ miles) N of Verona, northbound road to Cuzzano-Grezzana

open: By appointment only
open: As above

Further information from:
loc. Cuzzano, 37023 Grezzana
(VR)
Tel: 045 907045

Nearby sights of interest:
City of Verona, including Giardino
Giusti, the cathedral, Piazza delle
Erbe and Piazza dei Signori, the
Arche Sacligere, Castelvecchio e
Ponte Scaligero, the church of San
Zeno Maggiore, and the Arena.

The swirling garden below the
Villa Allegri Arvedi remains
almost as it was when laid in
the 17th century.

At Villa Allegri Arvedi it is astonishing to find a 17th-century
Veneto garden almost intact. What makes it remarkable is the
garden's relatively diminutive scale and its reliance upon the
surrounding extensive landscape to increase its apparent size –
for the real extent is limited to a *broderie* terrace and a short axial
approach road. The villa is set upon a broad terrace at the foot of
a wooded hillside, and is connected to the road by a spine of
crenellated hedging thrust boldly across the *vigna*. The visitor
progresses up the drive, passing the serried ranks of sculpted
cypress and box, enclosed in an avenue of persimmon trees
(Disopyros khaki), and is then funnelled into a courtyard,
overlooked by the family chapel, and thence into the house.
From the first floor balcony the majesty of the carefully
composed panorama is overwhelming: a great swirling *broderie* of
immaculate box arabesques, relieved by a central oval basin and
dozens of smooth sentinels of clipped box and cypress laid over a
terrace of gravel and bare earth, beyond which lies the open
countryside. Unlike most gardens, the box is kept low in the
17th-century manner, enhancing the clarity of the composition.

The present villa was built to the designs of G.B. Bianchi in
the mid 17th century. The box in the parterre was once thought
to have been modern, but dendrochronology has proven that it is
original. At one end of the terrace there is a *stanzone* containing
two artificial grottoes encrusted with *pietra spugnosa* stalactites.

Villa Barbarigo Pizzoni Ardemani

Location: 19km (11¾ miles) SW of Padua, take SS 16 for Bataglia Terme, then follow signs to Galzignano Terme and Valsanzibio

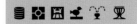

open: 1 Mar to 30 Nov, 9am–12pm, 2pm–sunset

Further information from:
35030 Valsanzibio di Galzignano (PD)
Tel: 049 9130042 and 049 9130029

Nearby sights of interest:
city of Padua, including the Basilica del Santo; the Brenta Canal.

It has been written of Villa Barbarigo Pizzoni Ardemani: "Consider an amphitheatre in the hills, the ends linked by a great avenue flung across the valley, and in this arrangement of lesser avenues furnished with all the delights of an Italian garden, box hedges, lemon trees, sculpture, pools and fountains, and you have an impression of the gardens at Valsanzibio." The first glimpse of the garden is through the Portale de Diana, an imposing triumphal arch set in a swampy hollow: you can then perceive a chain of majestic stepped fishponds, each terminating in rockworks and cascades surmounted by sculpture, that rise imperceptibly and appear to merge with the foothills behind. Once within the garden, the view to the villa from the *viale centrale* is framed by 4m (13ft) high box hedges, behind which lie the principal garden compartments, including the Rabbit Island, the Labyrinth, the prospect mount, and the stepped rosary. The gardens are a riot of waterworks, including cunningly concealed water games, which sprout from the base of benches to soak the unsuspecting visitor. There are over 120 different species of trees grown in the gardens, many of which are conifers planted in the 19th century.

The Portale de Diana makes an imposing entrance to the late 17th-century garden of the Villa Barbarigo Pizzoni Ardemani.

The great ensemble at Valsanzibio was formed in the late 17th century by Antonio Barbarigo, Procurator of San Marco, Venice, who conceived the landscape as an allegorical representation of a primeval Eden regained on earth. The gardens have also traditionally served as a place for botanical and medical research, and for mechanical and hydraulic innovations. That it retains its charm and character is a tribute to the present owner, Count Fabio Pizzoni Ardemani, an informed garden-lover, who over the past two decades has meticulously restored his estate and kept the gardens to a standard virtually unrivalled in Italy. Among the Count's most admirable improvements are the restoration of the Rabbit Island and the repair of 16 fountains, 3 *scherzi d'acqua* and 4 fishponds.

open: Spring to autumn, Tue and Sun, 2.30pm–6.30pm, weekdays by appointment
open: As above

Further information from:
13 Castello del Catajo, 35041 Battaglia Terme (PD)
Tel: 39 49 526541

Nearby sights of interest:
The town of Monsélice and the city of Padua.

Castello del Catajo

Location: 17km (10½ miles) SW of Padua, take SS 16 for Monsélice

Built in 1570–73, this extraordinary and atypical Venetian *maison de plaisance* in the Gothic taste stands on the edge of the Euganean hills. The portcullis opens into a court, known as the Court of the Giants on account of the frescoes which once embellished its walls. At one end is a splendid stairway that leads up to a flagged court planted with tall conifers. To the left there is an artificial grotto with lifesize animals and figures. Beyond the outer curtain wall of the *castello* are several garden compartments. Despite being rather forlorn they possess a collection of stately *Magnolia grandiflora*. The trees are aligned in impressive avenues along both sides of the long water, making a handsome display in the terraced garden on the south side of the castle. The remains of a small 18th-century pool and a scattering of sepulchral monuments can be found in the undergrowth.

open: 1 Apr to 30 Jun, Thu, Sat, 2pm–7pm, Sun and public holidays 10am–7pm; 1 Sep to 31Oct, Thu and Sat 2pm–6pm Sun and public holidays 10am–6pm; groups by appointment
open: As above

Further information from:
Loc. Rivella, 35043 Monsélice (PD)
Tel: 0429 781970 and 781987

Nearby sights of interest:
The town of Monsélice and the city of Padua.

Villa Emo

Location: From Padua 18km (11¼ miles) SS 16 or Autostrada A 13 exit Terme Euganee or Monsélice

This garden not only has a very strong design structure but, unusually for Italy, it is also full of flowers. Hornbeam tunnels, clipped hedges, fishponds with water plants, avenues of evergreen magnolias, herbaceous borders, vibrant rosebeds, and a *soigné* parterre of box and gravel below the façade of the elegant villa, are all immaculately maintained.

Built in 1588 and attributed to Palladio's pupil, Vincenzo Scamozzi, the villa has been extensively restored and the garden created since 1966 by the owner, Contessa Giuseppina Emo, and by her daughter, Marina Emo, who has lived here since 1980. A double staircase leads up to the classical portico where corinthian columns, their capitals in terracotta, make an imposing entrance to the almost cube-shaped villa, and provides a view over the patterned box in the centre of which a 17th-century stone pool and fountain has been incorporated.

Although most of the lines in the garden are straight, reflecting the Italianate influence and establishing a link with any garden layout that may have existed in the 16th century, much of the planting is delightfully informal with many indigenous flowers – primroses, hellebores and hepaticas from the local woods, mixed with meadow salvias *(Salvia pratensis)* and white-flowered *Iris orientalis*, and clumps of white arums

The Villa Emo has been restored and a new flower garden created.

(Zantedeschia aethiopica), growing in the water. Double herbaceous borders, inspired by frequent visits to England, are full of rich colour, with blocks of blue *Iris germanica* making a repetitive rhythm between robust perennials.

Situated in gently rolling countryside backed by the Euganean Hills, family-owned apple orchards and fields of corn and vineyards, the whole ensemble is delightful.

---

5 *Lake Garda: Villa Bettoni*

Location: Gargnano, 40km (25 miles) N of Brescia

Of all the villas on the Italian lakes few enjoy a more dramatic setting than the Villa Bettoni. Mountains rise behind the villa to form a breath-taking backdrop. The garden – although not open to the public – is entirely open to view, lying behind a wrought-iron screen and laid out as an architectural set-piece in the form of an amphitheatre, recessed from the road by a large *patte d'oie* that radiates from a central *piazzale*. Beyond a parterre, the confection is criss-crossed by double flights of ramps studded with grottoes, niches, sculptures, fountains, and balustrades that link a series of terraces and four temple-fronted lemon garden terraces. The composition culminates in a single flight of steps leading to a fountain enclosed by a wall inset with niches and urns. The park lies beyond the summit. The garden was built in 1764–68 and is a tribute to the tradition of lemon growing in the 18th and 19th centuries on the western shores of Lake Garda.

⊞ open: Not open to public and visible from the roadside only

Further information from:
Gargnano (BS)

Nearby sights of interest:
Town of Gargnano; Gardone Riviera; resort of Toscolano-Maderno; town of Brescia; environs of Lake Garda (by boat).

Sloping ramps studded with niches and grottoes link a series of terraces in the Baroque garden at Villa Bettoni.

open: 15 Mar to 15 Oct, daily, 9am–6pm

Further information from:
Via Motta 2, 25083 Gardone Riviera (BS)
Tel: 0336 410877

Nearby sights of interest:
Gardone Riviera, including Gabriele d'Annunzio's house and museum at Vitoriale; resort of Brescia; town of Salò; Toscolano-Maderno; environs of Lake Garda (by boat).

The botanic garden of Hruska is bisected with water rills between rocky outcrops, and planted with a wide range of exotics.

6 *Lake Garda: Giardino Hruska Botanico*

Location: 30km (18½ miles) from Brescia SS 11, to Rezzato then SS 45

This curious and compact garden is a botanical microcosm artfully contrived in a Dolomitic landscape. The sloping site amid rocky outcrops was laid out between 1910–71 by Dr Arturo Hruska, dentist to Nicholas II, last Czar of Russia. A riot of subtropical, alpine and desert flora intermingle to form a quirky assemblage that is characteristic of the best of the exotic gardens on the Italian lakes. Spectacular bristling groves of green and black bamboo *(Phyllostachys viridis* and *P. nigra)* thrive in the lee of stately cypresses, camphor trees, and cedars, that tower over beds of cacti and succulents – mostly planted in pots and including American agave and *Hylocereus undatus* – as well as sprawling colonies of alpines, ferns, bananas, reeds, lilies, and hydrangeas. Many of the garden furnishings, including gates, benches and bridges, are made from bamboo growing in the garden. Of special interest is the pair of black grotesque spouting masks that face each other across a pool in a bamboo grove. The garden was purchased in 1988 by the artist Andre Heller and has since become a setting for contemporary installations by Keith Haring, Roy Lichtenstein and Mimmo Palladino.

Villa Manin

Location: On SS 13, 30km (18½ miles) from Udine to Codroipo, then follow signs

The curving milky white wings – almost semi-circular *barchesse*, clearly inspired by Bernini's colonnade at St Peter's in Rome – of this 18th-century villa, spread out from the main façade to float like a mirage in the vast Friuli plain. Two great *columbaie* shelter the entrance, framing formal fishponds, and the open courtyard of grass. Napoleon, who signed the Treaty of Campoformido here in 1797, felt the palace, built like a miniature Versailles, was too rich and sumptuous to be a private residence. Today the arrival is still magical, although the garden has a desolate air. The villa is a centre for Friuli culture.

The villa, designed by Domenico Rossi, was begun in the early 18th century for Ludovico Manin, the last Doge of Venice, but was then altered and embellished during the 19th century. The garden was decorated with statues by Giuseppe Toretto. After 1863 the northern part of the garden was transformed into a romantic park, rich in specimen trees, and with historical and mythological themes. There are tulip trees and ginkgos, white pines (*Pinus strobus* from North America) and the Bhutan pine *(Pinus wallichiana)* from the Himalayas. Two strange mounds in the ground represent Etna and Parnassus – once accompanied by allegorical statuary.

open: Easter to 31 Oct, winter 9am–12am, 2pm–5pm, summer 9am–12.30pm, 3pm–6pm

open: All year except Jan, Tue to Sun

Further information from:
33030 Passariano (UD)
Tel: 0432 906657

Nearby sights of interest:
The old quarter of Pordenone; the town of Udine, including the Piazza della Libertà.

At the great Villa Manin the landscape park behind the house is an open meadow filled with daffodils.

open: Apr to Oct, daily,
9am–1pm, 3pm–6pm; Nov to Mar,
9am–1pm, closed Sunday
afternoons and holidays

Further information from:
Via Orto Botanico 15, 35100
Padua

Nearby sights of interest:
In Padua: Basilica del Santo,
including equestrian statue of
Gattamelata by Donatello,
frescoes by Giotto in the Cappella
degli Scrovegni, Palazzo della
Ragione, and Piazza dei Signori.
Near Padua: Brenta Riviera.

The Giardino Botanico in Padua,
laid out in the 16th century, still
retains much of its geometry
with additional planting around
the edge.

8 *Padua: Giardino Botanico*

Location: Behind the Basilica del Santo in the city centre

Of great historical and botanical interest the gardens, founded in
1545 as an apothecary's teaching garden for the medical school of
the University, are amongst the oldest in Europe.

The establishment of the gardens, as conceived by the
naturalist doctor Francesco Bonafede, the first holder of the
Chair *Lectrum Simplicium*, in order that living plants could be
studied, was ratified by the Venetian republic in May 1545. The
circular wall was started in 1551 to enclose the order beds; iron
gates and balustrading are of a later date. Today an outer wall
and buildings enclose further planting of trees and shrubs as well
as the circular walled garden.

Like other botanical gardens of Europe laid out in the middle
of the 16th century, the Padua garden reflected a new scientific
interest in classification of plants and natural products used in
herbal medicine. The garden certainly owes much to the interest
of the Venetian patrician and scholar, Daniele Barbaro (1514–17),
in the relationship between architecture and mathematics. He
was aided by the architect Giovanni Moroni from Bergamo.
Unusually at Padua the rectangle, divided as a quadrant,
enclosed inside the circular wall, was further sub-divided into
ornate and complicated squares and circles of geometrical
complexity. Goethe, on his visit to the gardens in 1786, first saw

the European fan palm *(Chamaerops humilis)* that stimulated his search for the "original" plant from which all others have evolved, thus anticipating the theory of evolution. Several exotic plants when introduced to Europe were first grown in the botanic gardens, including lilac *(Syringa vulgaris),* sunflowers *(Helianthus annuus),* the potato *(Solanum tuberosum),* and jasmine *(Jasminum fruticans).*

Villa Pisani

Location: 25 km (15½ miles) from Venice, along the Brenta Canal, following signs for Mira-Strà

open: Daily except Mon
9am–1.30pm
open: As above

Further information from:
Via A. Pisani 6, 30039 Strà (VE)
Tel: 049 9800590

Nearby sights of interest:
Town of Strà; boat trip along the Brenta Canal; cities of Padua and Venice.

Gates along the Brenta Canal, one with a triumphal arch, give grandeur to the setting of Villa Pisani, and remind today's visitor that the 18th-century traveller would have arrived by water and had a first glimpse of the garden through the massive portico. Today the façade of the villa is surrounded by gentle lawns and trees visible from the road. Decorative statues still abound topping the high walls and flanking the "modern" canal (1911).

This imposing 18th-century palace and stables was rebuilt on the site of a 16th-century family residence between 1730–40. The layout of the park, with great rides through the fields and forest, terminated by handsome gates and iron grills allowing further views into the countryside, show French influence. Other features include a labyrinth of high hedges, with a small circular tower and statue of Minerva, an elegant hexagonal archway centred where six forest rides meet, and a mount with wide steps leading to a pavilion or coffee house, once surrounded by a moat.

At Villa Pisani the long canal between the stables and the villa is 20th century. The stables retain their original Frigimelica facade, dating from about 1730.

open: All year by appointment from the Administrazione Guerrieri Rizzardi (045 7210288); Apr to Oct, Sat 11am–7pm

Further information from: Poiega, 37024 Negrar (VR)

Nearby sights of interest: City of Verona; environs of Lake Garda.

At the Villa Rizzardi the green theatre, designed by Luigi Trezza in 1796, still retains tiered seats of box, backed by a hedge of hornbeam.

Giardino di Villa Rizzardi

Location: Negrar, 18km (11 miles) from Verona by SS 12 for Trento and Pescantina

The most memorable feature of the gardens of Villa Rizzardi is the green theatre, the finest of its kind in Italy. It was designed by Luigi Trezza in 1796; he had completed the rest of the remarkable garden between 1783–91 for Conte Antonio Rizzardi. Today it is a rare treasure, incorporating many of the geometrical features of classical Renaissance gardens.

The villa itself was rebuilt at the end of the 19th century, but most of the garden features survive. Basically the gardens lie on three main levels on a slope above the main building. Trezza aligned the cross alleys and vistas to catch views of hills and mountains at every turn. A small private garden behind the house is reached from the *piano nobile* by a bridge, with fountains and box borders leading to a shady alley of clipped hornbeam. Another parallel alley of *Ostrya carpinifola* makes high hedges of green, almost forming a complete arbour, and making a line of sunlight. An avenue of cypresses, interspersed with palm trees, leads up the hill to a belvedere, beside a wilder *bosco*, where stone wild beasts lurk in the undergrowth. The theatre, still used for performances, has tiers of seats contoured against the hillside, cut out in boxwood, and backed by hornbeam and fine statues.

Trieste: Castello di Miramare

Location: 10km (6¼ miles) NW of Trieste

open: Daily, winter, 9am–5pm, summer 9am–7pm
open: Daily, winter, 9am–4pm, summer 9am–6pm

Further information from:
34014 Grignano, Trieste (TS)
Tel: 040 224143

Nearby sights of interest:
Seaport of Trieste. Near Trieste: Villa Opicina and the Grotta Gigante.

Built in Istrian stone between 1856–60 for the Archduke Maximilian of Austria and his wife Charlotte, the neo-gothic castle retains its original furnishings. A formal Italian-style garden, with annuals and roses planted inside box-edged beds, has terraces descending to the shore, on the bay of Grignano.

A pergola clothed with wisteria leads from near the castle to the romantic landscape park. With the help of the landscape gardener Antonio Jelinek, a forest of Austrian pine *(Pinus nigra)* was established as a windbreak to the east, allowing species of bamboo, *Chamaerops humilis*, scented *Pittosporum tobira*, oleanders, and paulownias to flourish, and native *macchia* of bay laurel, arbutus, and myrtle to regenerate. Today dense woods of pines and holm oak shelter the magnificent property. The Archduke helped to finance the explorations of Alexander von Humboldt of 1857–59, and rare American agaves, araucarias from Brazil, and aloes were acquired. Even during his ill-fated expedition to Mexico, Maximilian sent Mexican and Californian plants back to Miramare, the garden of which was his real interest.

The Archduke Maximilian was able to indulge his interest in plant collecting at Miramare. A formal garden lies below the neo-gothic castle.

12 *Villa Trissino Marzotto*

Location: 18km (11¼ miles) W of Vicenza, take A 4 motorway, exit Montecchio Maggiore, then take SS 246 towards Valdagno

open: By appointment only

open: As above

Further information from:
Piazza Trissino 2, 36070
Trissino (VI)
Tel and fax: 0445 962029

Nearby sights of interest:
City of Vicenza; Monte Berico Basilica; Villa Valmarina "ai Nana"; Rotonda (Villa Capra); city of Verona.

The gardens of the Villa Trissino Marzotto have many interesting features, with soaring cypresses dominating buildings and layout.

The silhouette of Villa Marzotto and its extensive grounds bristling with towering cypresses forms a conspicuous landmark on the skyline of Trissino. After ascending through the town to Piazza Trissino the visitor turns into the spacious courtyard of the villa. What catches the eye is not, however, the palace, but the broad terrace to the right, which is terminated by a giant ashlar screen surmounted with exuberant finials that forms both a turning radius and a *claire-voyée*. Here there is a choice of ascending to the 15th-century villa (recast in the 19th century) or decanting into the long south-facing terrace. The latter is probably the best choice, as from the hanging terrace the visitor gains a breathtaking panorama over the Montecchio countryside. The view is, moreover, framed by a crenellated yew hedge and a series of statues attributed to Orazio Marinali.

Progressing down along the terrace there is a second *rond-point*, this one encircled with majestic cypresses, but here the ground divided into a range of symmetrical Rococo figures,

outlined in low stone mouldings and crested with flamboyant cartouches. From this point there is a descent by a long drive through a wood of yew, hemlock, holly, spruce, holm oak, and box, with occasional glimpses of the park that lies on the north side of the hill. Gradually the views open out and a grassy plateau is reached upon which sits the ivyclad ruins of a former villa embowered by stately *Sophora japonica*, *Gleditsia triacanthos*, *Cercis siliquastrum*, *Sequoiadendron giganteum*, *Pinus wallichiana*, and *Cedrus libani* ssp. *atlantica*. There a surprise awaits – just below the forlorn surroundings of the ruin is a colossal balustraded terrace, in immaculate order, at the centre of which is an octangular pool, known as the "Laghetto del Marinali". The entrance gate to the lower villa is an eccentric and grandiose confection of porticos and free-standing columns supporting trophies.

13 *Verona: Giardino Giusti*

Location: Via Giusti, on the west bank of the River Adige

open: Daily, summer
8am–8pm, winter 8am–sunset

Set on a steep hillside behind the villa courtyard, the garden, with its *viale* of cypresses leading from the gateway between clipped parterres to an underground grotto and a high belvedere, comes as a complete surprise to the visitor. On the highest level, where citrus and pomegranates originally grew on terraces, there is now thick 19th-century landscape-style planting, in which the original grotesque stone masks seem perfectly at home. Below, on the flat, formal box-edged parterres, lemons in pots, and fountains, convey a more ordered air to match the main cypress walk and cross axes of single cypresses. This is one of the oldest Renaissance gardens in northern Italy, probably laid out in the 1570s. The original labyrinth was redesigned by the architect Luigi Trezza in 1786 – and has recently been reinstated. The elaborate geometric parterre of box on the flat area in front of the hill was also "renovated" in the 18th century.

The garden has been much visited. The diarist John Evelyn came in 1644 and Goethe was inspired by the "huge cypresses which soar into the air like awls". The American architect Charles Platt, who noted the poor state of the garden at the end of the 1800s, would be reassured by today's excellent maintenance and new plantings of quiet flowers and suitable groundcovers. There are unspoilt views to the Tyrol Alps and across the Po to Mantua.

Further information from:
Via Giusti 2, 37129 Verona
Tel: 045 8034029

Nearby sights of interest:
City of Verona, including Piazza delle Erbe, Piazza dei Signori, Arche Scaligere, Castelvecchio e Ponte Scaligero; Chiesa di San Zeno Maggiore, and the Arena.

The Giardino Giusti, on the hillside above the River Adige in Verona, keeps its 16th-century outline, although the parterres were remodelled in French style in the 18th century.

Key to gardens

1 Giardino Buonaccorsi
2 Castello di Celsa
3 Villa Chigi Cetinale
4 Le Balze
5 Bobili Garden
6 Villa Capponi
7 Castello Gardens
8 Parco Celle
9 Palazzo Corsini
10 Villa Gamberaia
11 Villa Guicciardini Corsi Salviati

12 Villa Medici
13 Villa della Petraia
14 Villa La Pietra
15 Villa Pratolino
16 Giardino dei Semplici
17 Villa i Tatti
18 Villa La Foce
19 Villa Garzoni
20 Villa Mansi
21 Villa Reale
22 Villa Massei

23 Villa Torrigiani
24 Villa Caprile
25 Villa Imperiale
26 Villa Miralfiore
27 Palazzo Piccolomini
28 Orto Botanico, Pisa
29 Certosa di Pontignano
30 Venzano

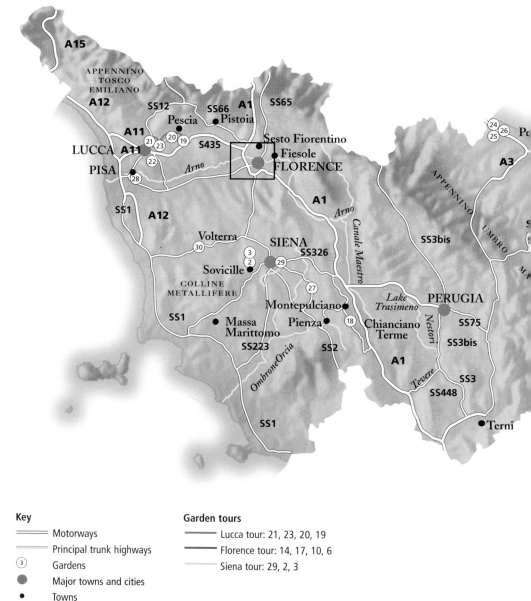

Key

═══ Motorways
─── Principal trunk highways
③ Gardens
⬤ Major towns and cities
• Towns

Garden tours

─── Lucca tour: 21, 23, 20, 19
─── Florence tour: 14, 17, 10, 6
─── Siena tour: 29, 2, 3

Tuscany & the Marches

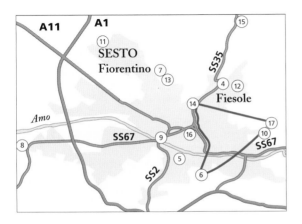

ANCONA

ena¹

●Civitanova Marche

A14

In central northern Italy there are striking differences in climate that are related to the proximity of the Apennines (and, of course, the altitude) and the coast. In the regions around Florence winters are severe and summers hot, while near Lucca and Pisa the climate is far milder and wetter, and on the eastern side of the Apennines and western strip of the Adriatic, conditions are relatively benign.

All through the Middle Ages the main Tuscany region was devoted to agriculture in fairly small estates. The Tuscan countryside still has an enormous number of villas, farmhouses and gardens, with fields cultivating vines, and grain, and terraced olive groves, each setting dominated by typical tall cypresses. Tuscan gardens need to be appreciated with their surrounding landscapes of which they are a part. For the foreigner this has always been part of their charm. By the end of the 15th century the Medicis, from the Mugello Hills north of Florence, had become in economic terms one of the most important families in Europe, acting as patrons to artists and sculptors, owning many properties, and converting

The gardens to be seen in the city of Florence.

medieval dwellings into new style Renaissance villas, often designed by Michelozzi but much influenced by the writing of Leon Battista Alberti. The latter's humanistic concepts, developed in *De Re Aedificatore* (1452), praised life in the villa, according to his studies of Roman texts, but also advised on the suitability of a site and the structure for a villa. By the 1550s, the Medici Grand Dukes had engaged Tribolo, Ammanati and Buontalenti to create settings with strict iconographical programmes. These, based on classical mythology, were often related to the family's achievement and grandeur. The purity and repose of the earlier gardens was disturbed by elaborate water jokes – the famous *giochi d'acqua* – and theatrical presentations, the features and themes of which were copied throughout Italy and northern Europe. The architect Baldassare Peruzzi (1481–1537) worked in both Rome and in and around Siena, bringing innovative ideas from Rome when he returned to Siena in 1527. However, in the Marche, under Vatican rule for many centuries, the villa gardens were mainly influenced by developments in Rome. Along the plain near Lucca, at the base of the Apian alps, gardens of great quality were developed from the early 17th century. The four great gardens, the Villa Mansi (p.81), Villa Garzoni (p.81), Villa Marlia (p.82), and Villa Torrigiani (p.84), are more worthy of today's excursion, with the Baroque water garden and theatre at Marlia, combining with Elisa Baciocchi's landscape park, one of the high points of an Italian garden tour.

The Medici were not only builders and patrons of art, but as plant collectors were instrumental in establishing the botanic gardens of Pisa and Florence. Today, the plant collections being re-established in the Boboli Garden, and in the Medici villas at Castello and Petraia, reflect that interest.

The secret garden at the Villa Torrigiani in Lucca dates to the early 17th century with a *ninfeo* of tufa stone.

Giardino Buonaccorsi

Location: 25km (15½ miles) from Macerata; take the A 14 and exit Civitanova Marche, 11 km (7 miles)

open: Mar to Sep, Sat 8am–12pm; preferably groups by appointment

open: As above

Further information from:
Via Giardino 9 62018 Potenza Picena, Macerata
Tel: 0733 880355

Nearby sights of interest:
Loreto; Recanati.

The early 18th-century Giardino Buonaccorsi is laid out on a series of south-facing terraces that still retain their original flowerbed pattern.

This garden, on a hill overlooking the sea, is unique in Italy in so far as it is virtually unchanged since it was originally laid out in the first decade of 18th century. Although not on the tourist's or garden visitor's normal itinerary, it is well worth a detour. The Buonaccorsi who commissioned the villa had many cardinals in the family, and owned a magnificent palace in Macerata, designed by Contini, who probably also designed the garden. On the east of the villa, in front of the chapel, we can admire the only perfectly preserved flower garden in Italy. The garden is laid out on five descending terraces to the south east of the villa, sheltered by hedges from the wind and warmed by the southern exposure to provide ideal growing conditions for lemons. The main axis, edged with masks from the Commedia d'Arte, leads through a stair from the niche decorated with mosaics containing the statue of the Fauno Suonatore (Playing Faun) onto the upper terrace to the Grotto of the Shepherd. Four compartments with curved sides at the centre define an elliptical space. Small quadrangular and hexagonal stone-edged beds form a pattern around an obelisk, sited on a Baroque pedestal in a star-shaped bed. The pattern of the layout comes from Ferrari's *De Florum Cultura* (1637).

On the second terrace sixteen compartments, hedged with *plates-bandes* for annuals, repeat the curved pattern, thus defining small squares with a central obelisk. At every corner lemon pots are placed on stone pedestals in diagonal positions, enhancing the Baroque movement of the space. The middle terrace is known as the "Alley of the Caesars" for its statues of Roman emperors. The garden still has 149 statues, representing classic or grotesque figures, from the Venetian workshop of Orazio Marinali, who signed one of the sculptures. Once there were many *giochi d'acqua* but today only those in the small square in the centre of the Alley of the Caesars still function.

Castello di Celsa

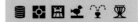

Location: Celsa, SW of Siena, 10km (6½ miles) N of Sovicille on SS 73

The foundations of Celsa, owned by the Aldobrandini family, date to the 13th or 14th century, when the building may well have resembled one of those castles depicted in the romantic landscapes of Martini that hang in the Palace of the Commune in Siena. Isolated in the oak and chestnut woods, it was transformed into a villa in the early 16th century but was partly destroyed in 1554 by Austro-Spanish troops and then restored in the 17th century. Later it was rebuilt in Gothic revival style.

The original 16th-century garden at Celsa was designed by Baldassare Peruzzi (1481–1537), although all that remains of his work is the circular chapel that stands in the corner of the formal garden. The garden was altered when the villa was restored in the 17th century, with an imposing new entrance gateway and a balustraded semi-circular pool hanging over the valley from which the distant towers of Siena can be seen. More recently, a simple gravel and box parterre was introduced to represent the Aldobrandini coat of arms.

Another distinguished feature of the garden is the pool set in the woods at some distance from the *castello*. A 17th-century design shows the elegant balustraded pool approached by steep steps – three avenues radiate into the forest from it. Today it is approached through a hayfield of wild flowers flanked with trimmed swags of cypress and topiary balls.

open: By appointment only, for groups of ten or more. Contact Livia Pediconi Aldobrandini, Piazza dei Coprettari, 70,Rome 00186
Tel: 06 686 1138
Fax: 06 6830 7326
open: As above

Further information from:
2 Castello di Celsa, 53018
Sovicille, Siena
Tel: 0577 317002

Nearby sights of interest:
Siena; Villa Chigi Cetinale; Castello di Belcaro, Monteriggioni.

At the Castello di Celsa the box and gravel parterre in the hanging garden beside Peruzzi's chapel represents the Aldobrandini coat of arms.

open: By appointment only
open: As above

Further information from:
53098 Sovicille, Siena
Tel: 0577 311147
Fax: 0577 311061

Nearby sights of interest:
City of Siena; Castello di Celsa;
Castello di Belcaro; fortress-village
of Monteriggioni.

Villa Chigi Cetinale

Location: 14km (8¾ miles) SW of Siena; take SS 73 for Massa Maritima and then
signposts for Sovicille and Anciano

Backed by a steep hill and thick forests of oak, noble Cetinale has a dramatic setting, looking over a valley of gentle farmland. East-west axial views through the villa are aligned on a vast statue of Hercules across a ravine and on the Hermitage or *Romitorio* on the hill's summit. The villa, expanded in the 17th century from a humbler farmhouse to become a symbol of the power and prestige of the famous banking Chigi family of Siena, has, with its gardens, been immaculately restored and enriched by Lord Lambton and Mrs Ward over the past twenty years. Cetinale combines historical features and authenticity with a 17th-century design by Carlo Fontana – the long western *allée* opening out to a natural amphitheatre at the base of the hill –

The view from the villa looking over
the Italian garden, which probably
dates to the 19th century.

The villa towers above the
English garden in which wisteria,
roses, irises, and peonies perform.

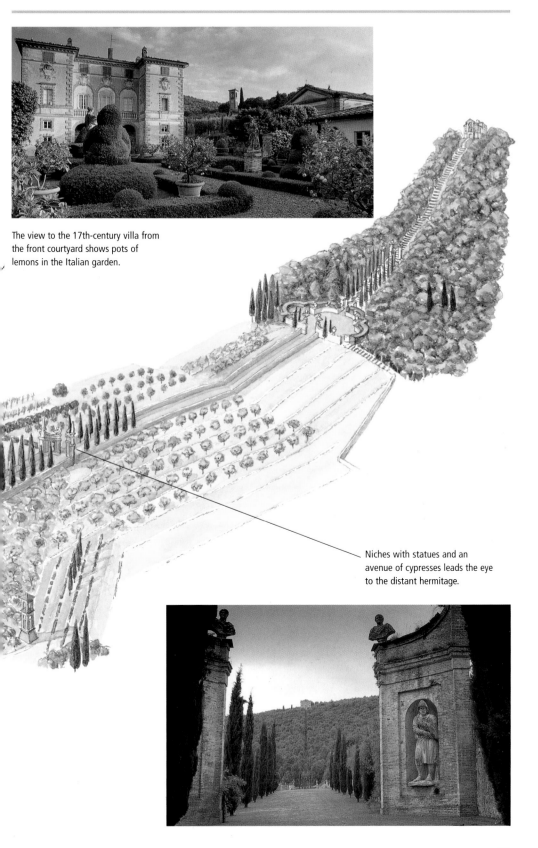

The view to the 17th-century villa from the front courtyard shows pots of lemons in the Italian garden.

Niches with statues and an avenue of cypresses leads the eye to the distant hermitage.

Irises in flower in May border one of the paths in the English Garden below the villa.

From the theatre looking back at the villa. This was the original arrival road from Siena.

and the extraordinary Thebaid or Holy Wood with a series of votive chapels and statues of hermits conceived by Cardinal Flavio Chigi, a 19th-century "Italian garden" – box-edged beds and lemons in pots – around the house, and a flower garden below the south façade in which wisteria, roses, peonies, perennials and bulbs, as well as vegetables, flourish in geometric beds separated by gravel paths, giving a luxuriant English look even in the heat of summer.

The Chigi pope, Alexander VII (1655–67), spent much of his youth in the farmhouse at Cetinale, bequeathing it to his nephew Flavio. The latter employed the Roman architect Fontana, a pupil of Bernini, to extend the house, adding a double marble staircase on the west façade and the great door with, above it, the Chigi Coats of Arms: the papal mitre and the keys of the Kingdom of Heaven. On the south side protruding wings joined by an open loggia (later filled in) extended the villa. Fontana also designed the chapel, *limonaia*, and *fattoria* on either side of the main entrance. The grandest part of the new garden is to the west, where he introduced a walled grass *allée*, the width of the new double staircase, stretching to a pair of brick gate piers, in the niches of which are crammed a pair of 15th-century copies of the Romanian figures on Trajan's column in Rome. Beyond the piers the walk is narrowed but continues sloping gently up to the "theatre", framed by a bust of Napoleon and one of his marshalls (Napoleon is supposed to have visited Cetinale in 1811), and narrows again to begin the ascent of 200 steps to the hermitage on the hilltop. The original arrival

entrance will have been from the old Siena road, winding around the base of the hillside into the area now called the theatre but then a forecourt lined with busts, allowing a view down to the villa with its splendid new marble stairway. Fontana's five-storey hermitage, faced with a cross of Lorraine, was finished in 1713. Lord Lambton acquired the hermitage in 1990 and it is now being restored. The view from the skyline makes the climb worthwhile but is best made by a track that winds around the hillside. Fontana's plans did not include the cypress *allée* which is a later addition. There are 17th-century plans of the villa that show a proposed parterre garden to the south of the walled walk – although this may never have been implemented.

In the Italian Garden on the other side of the house statues by Giuseppe Mazzuoli and lemons, with Portugal laurel and evergreen viburnums, give architectural definition to the box-edged beds. An avenue of clipped ilex runs east to the Mazzuoli statue of Hercules, symbol of Chigi power. The "penitentiary" to the north, with green rides striking through the woods, are part of Cardinal Flavio's penance and repentance for a misspent youth, with votive chapels decorated with frescoes representing the Seven Sorrows of the Virgin. Haunted by spirits and peopled with wild boar the woods are dark and mysterious. Joseph Forsyth visited the Chigi villa in 1800 and his description still seems appropriate: "Cetinale, which lies in a wide scraggy oakwood about ten miles from Siena, owes its rise and celebrity to the remorse of an amorous cardinal, who, to appease the ghost of a murdered rival, transformed a gloomy plantation of cypress into a penitential Thebaid, and acted there all the austerities of an Egyptian hermit." The theme of the Thebaid refers to the communities of the Desert Fathers around the ancient city of Thebes in the first centuries after Christ. The famous Palio of Siena was run in the Thebiad 16 times between 1690–1710 because of riots in the city. Mazzuoli carvings of winning *contrade* – a winged dragon, tortoises, a snail, a viper, and a porpoise head – can be found in the undergrowth along the paths.

In the early years of this century a Chigi marquis had an English mother, Mrs Elliot, who probably began the charming flower gardening below the villa. The old cypresses may not be in Fontana's plan, but casting dark shadows across the anemone-strewn grass between the olive terraces, they symbolize the Englishman's dream of the Italian garden. Nowadays, Cetinale, restored and recreated, owes its new life and vigour to its dedicated custodians.

The clock tower in the olive groves on the slope above the villa.

4

Florence: Le Balze

Location: Fiesole, 8km (5 miles) N of Florence

open: All year, by appointment only
open: As above

Further information from:
Via Vecchia Fiesolana 26, 50014 Fiesole, Florence
Tel: 055 59208

Nearby sights of interest:
Fiesole, including the Cathedral, Roman theatre, Monastery of San Francesco; Florence.

Pinsent designed the grotto to resemble a Renaissance garden.

Le Balze was designed by the British architect Cecil Pinsent for the American philosopher Charles Augustus Strong and built between 1912–13. The narrow space available was skilfully arranged by Pinsent, enhancing the feeling of depth and spreading the garden laterally. Parallel axes gave opportunity to create very long perspectives and a succession of garden rooms. The visitor, entering the first garden, glimpses the other spaces through openings in the walls. Eye-catchers, such as urns, statues and niches attract the eye and encourage further exploration.

The main garden, laid out in four compartments, is decorated with lemon pots. The panoramic view of Florence is screened with a wall, so that an arched window creates a delicate frame. On the northern side, a grotto decorated with tufa stone and shells recalls the late Renaissance garden grottos of Tuscany and Latium. Two stairs lead to an upper level from where the visitor can either descend to the *boschetto* of holm oaks or, walking eastward, can admire the main garden and the view of the town. The relationship between the house and the garden is strong with the long perspective of the main corridor, inspired by the Biblioteca of San Marco, continuing through another enclosed garden until a statue placed in a niche arrests the eye.

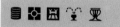

5

Florence: Boboli Garden

Location: behind the Pitti Palace, main entrance Piazza Pitti, in the city centre

open: All year, except the first and the last Mon of each month, daily, 9am–variable depending on season
open: Every day except Mons, 1 Jan, 1 May, 15 Aug, and Christmas 9am–2pm (9am–1pm Sun and public holidays); Pitti Palace, including Galleria Platina, Museo degli Argenti, Galleria d'Arte Moderna, and Galleria del Costume.

Further information from:
50125 Florence
Tel: 055 218741
Fax: 055 212397

Nearby sights of interest:
Florence, including churches of Santo Spirito and Santa Felìcita.

The Boboli is particularly remarkable for its history, its formal layout, architecture, fountains, grottoes and collection of Roman, Renaissance and Baroque sculptures. It was started in 1549 by the Duke Cosimo de' Medici (1519–1574) and his wife Eleonora di Toledo. The first part of the garden was designed by Tribolo. The main feature is the Amphitheatre, the site of a sandstone quarry used in the construction of the Pitti Palace and the Ponte Santa Trinità. It was originally terraced and planted with deciduous trees: planes, limes, chestnuts, field maples, elms, and oaks. Vasari, Ammanati and Buontalenti continued Tribolo's project, which was completed by 1579. In 1630–34 the green Amphitheatre was transformed, under the Grand Duke Ferdinando II and the architect Giulio Parigi, into a stone Amphitheatre with concentric steps where the audience could sit and watch performances. The garden had been enlarged in 1612 by Parigi. The vast area included within the medieval city walls (east) and the city (north west) was laid out on either sides of the Viale dei Cipressi, a long avenue that runs south of the Amphitheatre down the hill towards the Isolotto Basin. Here an island was created as a flower and lemon garden. In 1637 the Fontana dell' Oceano, made by Giambologna between 1574 and 1577, was moved from the Amphitheatre and placed at the centre of the island. Three large labyrinths, planted on the east side of the Viale dei Cipressi, were unfortunately destroyed in 1834 by the creation of a new carriage drive.

In spite of its long history the Boboli Garden preserves most of its original Renaissance and Baroque layout, except for the missing labyrinths. The fine collection of statues still remains. The most famous sculpture in the garden is the *Nano Morgante* by Valerio Cioli, a fat naked dwarf riding a tortoise, allegory of laziness and wisdom. Particularly precious are the two *Prigionieri Daci*, dating from the 3rd century AD. Any visit to the Boboli should also include the Grotto di Madama, built in 1554 by the architect David Fortini, and decorated with sculptures by Baccio Bandinelli and paintings by Bachiacca. But even more astonishing is the Grotto del Buontalenti, so named after its architect, a complex structure decorated with statues made of stalactites and tufa, representing the myth of Deucalione and Pirra. In the third room there is a marble *Venus* by Giambologna at the centre of small fountain. In the grotto a system of water drops and jets keep the air and the tufa sculptures humid; after restoration it will be open to the public in 1998.

A visit to the Limonaia Garden should not be missed during the summer months for the remarkable display of historic flowers, all of which have recently researched and replanted. In the Isolotto Garden (open in May and June) there is a collection of classic roses, also recently replanted.

The lemon garden at the Boboli Garden, known as the "Isolotto", is today planted with a collection of old roses.

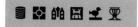

open: By appointment only
open: As above

Further information from:
Via del Pian dei Giullari, 3
Tel: 055 223 465

Nearby sights of interest:
Florence, including San Miniato church, Piazzale Michelangelo, Belvedere Fortress., Bobili Garden, Pitti Palace, Giardino dei Semplici, Santo Spirito church, Santa Felicita church, Ponte Vecchio, monuments of the Piazza del Duomo, and the Uffizi Museum.

At Villa Capponi the lower garden, added at the beginning of the 20th century, is planted out with annuals edged with box.

6 *Florence: Villa Capponi*

Location: Via del Pian de'Giullari, Arcetri, Florence

The gardens of Villa Capponi are amongst the most charming in the hills around Florence. It was much appreciated by Edith Wharton for its beautiful "oblong of old turf adjoining the house" and by Geoffrey Jellicoe for its "outdoor scented flower-rooms". Both features can still be appreciated. In 1572 the villa belonged to Gino do Lodovico Capponi. By the middle of the 18th century one walled garden had been built north of the house and another one, on a lower level, to the south. The small gardens, edged by tall walls with a Rococo curvilinear shape, ornamented with terracotta urns, are still perfectly preserved.

In 1882 the villa was purchased by Lady Elisabeth Scott, who added the two external loggias, built with columns from the medieval centre of Florence. At the beginning of the 20th century a new garden was attached on an even lower level to the south. In 1935 Cecil Pinsent was employed to add a further garden enclosd by cypress hedges, in which a swimming pool was hidden. At this time a variety of flowers were displayed in the box parterres and a mixed border was planted along the cypress hedge that shelters the lawn near the house. The present owner has simplified the planting scheme (myosotis in the north garden, *Viscaria elegans* in the south, tagetes along the cypress hedge).

Florence: Villa di Castello

Location: 5km (3 miles) N of Florence

The high Renaissance 16th-century gardens of Castello, made for Cosimo de' Medici, became the prototype for many other Italian gardens. Soon after his election as Duke of Tuscany in 1537, Cosimo decided to transform the old family palace into a grand villa and the orchards behind it into a garden. The garden was designed by Tribolo. The two fountains of Ercole e Anteo and Venus, respectively symbols of victory over tyranny and of eternal spring, allegorized Medici rule. The layout of the garden is still preserved, but the Venus was moved with the Ercole e Anteo group taking its place. The box hedges lining the paths were probably planted at the turn of 19th century. The most extraordinary feature of Castello is the Grotta degli Animali, started by Tribolo in 1550. Its walls are decorated with many animals, representing those saved from the Flood. Three marble basins are carved with garlands of shells and fishes.

More than 500 citrus plants are cultivated in pots and in another hidden garden are old varieties of roses and the rare *Jasminum sambac* 'Grand Duke of Tuscany'. Double stairways lead to the upper terrace, where in the middle of a holm oak wood is the pond of the Appennino or Inverno (Winter), a bronze statue modelled by Ammanati in 1564.

open: All year, except the second and third Mon of each month, daily 9.00am–variable depending on season

Further information from:
Via di Castello, 50141 Firenze
Tel: 055 454791
Fax: 055 212397

Nearby sights of interest:
City of Florence; Villa della Petraia and Villa di Poggio a Caiano.

The layout at the Castello Gardens is much as it was in the middle of the 15th century, and the collection of lemons has been restored.

71

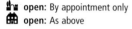

open: By appointment only
open: As above

Further information from:
Santa Omato, Pistoia
Tel: 0573 479338

Nearby sights of interest:
Town of Pistoia, including Piazza del Duomo, and the frieze in the Ospedale del Ceppo.

A sculpture of two pieces of a gigantic head at Parco Celle.

8 *Florence: Parco Celle*

Location: Via Montalese, Fattoria di Celle, Santomato, 6km (3¾ miles) from Pistoia

Today the old 17th-century formal garden remains on the south side of the villa and the landscape garden, created in the early 19th century, has become a site for displaying contemporary works of art. The present villa assumed its Baroque form in the second half of the 17th century for Cardinal Agostini Fabroni, who also added a beautiful chapel with Palladian portico and ordered formal gardens to be laid out on both the north and the south side of the villa. The lower south terrace, reached by a grand elliptical staircase, still contains two separate orange gardens, and an orchard on the west side.

In 1818 the villa was acquired by Count Caselli, who asked the architect Gambini to convert the formal garden to the north to a romantic park. The results are eclectic with a naturalistic lake, island and temple, waterfall and rustic bridge, and an Egyptian Monument. There is a fine neo-Gothic Temple of the Spring, designed by Ferdinando Marini. The estate was bought by Giuliano Gori in 1969, who started the "Art Spaces". These include a labyrinth by Robert Morris, an *ampiteatro* by Beverley Pepper, two pieces of a gigantic head transfixed by the arrows of Heracles and Apollo, the Teme II, and Variations by Fausto Meloti, a group of geometric metal sculptures rising from a lake.

open: By appointment only from 1 Apr to 1 Nov
open: As above

Further information from:
Via del Prato 58, 50123 Firenze
Tel: 055 218 994 (Mon, Wed and Fri 9.30am-12.30pm)
Fax: 055 268123

Nearby sights of interest:
City of Florence, including Santa Maria Novella, San Lorenzo, Palazzo Medici-Riccardi.

9 *Florence: Palazzo Corsini*

Location: Near the Porta al Prato in the north-west of the city

These gardens remain as a rare example of a late Renaissance town garden. Today, after recent restoration, geometric clipped box surrounds beds in which indigenous plants such as cistus, lavenders, santolinas, *Teucrium fruticans*, rosemary, catmint, and scented thymes are massed to give a charming effect. Specimens of the Japanese bitter orange, *Poncirus trifoliata*, with sweetly-scented white flowers, give height and bulk in the centre of the larger beds, and other exotic shrubs include magnolias *(Magnolia grandiflora)*, and the Chinese bead tree *(Melia azedarach)*.

From the loggia (1625–28) a double avenue of statues and large pots of lemons leads the eye to an entrance gate. The *viale* of statues is crossed by a series of axial views leading on the east side to a romantic *bosco* of evergreen oaks and hackberries *(Celtis australis)*, with paths flanked with hedges of *Laurus nobilus* and evergreen viburnums, and a profusion of periwinkle and acanthus, recalling the 19th-century Italian idea of the *giardino inglese*.

Florence: Villa Gamberaia

Location: Take No 10 bus past bridge over Mensola stream and up the hill

Gamberaia lies to the east of Florence in still almost unspoilt countryside, cultivated with olive groves and facing onto the Arno valley. It is one of the most celebrated Italian villas and, since its "restoration" in Edwardian times, the garden has been considered a masterpiece. The 15th-century villa was purchased by the Capponi family in 1718, who then enlarged the house, added fountains, statues, the grotto garden, and the bowling alley leading to the *nymphaeum* of Pan, the lemon garden, and orangery on an upper terrace. The main terrace was laid out with *parterres de broderie* and with a small elliptical rabbit island, the *conigliera*. In 1896, the villa was bought by Princess Kashko Caterina Ghyka who, together with her friend Mrs Blood, destroyed the parterres and *conigliera* and created four pools hedged with narrow beds for a large variety of flowers and, on the eastern side, a semicircular pool, hedged by arched clipped cypresses. Edith Wharton complained about the projects as "unrelated in style to its [sic] surroundings". In 1905, Princess Ghyka sold the villa to a wealthy American, Mrs Von Ketteler, who simplified the planting, improved the box hedges, the topiary shapes, and the yew pillars. In the early 1950s, the property was purchased by Marcello Marchi, who restored the villa and garden, both of which had been damaged during the war.

open: By appointment only
open: As above

Further information from:
Via del Rossellino 72, 50135
Florence
Tel: 055 697 205
Fax: 055 697 027

Nearby sights of interest:
Village of Settignano; the city of Florence.

At Gamberaia the layout was "reconstructed" in the early years of the 20th century. Panels of water are edged with box and narrow flowerbeds.

Florence : Villa Guicciardini Corsi Salviati

Location: in suburbs 9km (5½ miles) NW of Florence

open: By appointment only

Further information from:
Via Gramsci 462, 50019 Sesto
Fiorentino, Florence
Tel: 055 443805

Nearby sights of interest:
Florence, including Villa Medicea
di Castello, Villa Medicea della
Petraia, and Museo delle
Porcellane.

The Villa Guicciardini Corsi Salviati, although it is now almost part of the town of Sesto, is screened from the industrial landscape by a belt of trees. The villa and garden lie on the flat and a series of linked garden rooms are contained in a walled rectangular space behind the house. An old medieval palace was transformed into a villa in 1640. A further transformation was made in 1738 when the façades were decorated in Baroque style, and a new garden was laid out along the south side with a *claire-voyée* supported by pilasters ornamented with statues, and a circular pond with water jets. The original fishpond was converted into a rectangular canal. By 1815 a landscape garden had been created on the east side where, later, conservatories were erected for succulent and tropical plants.

After 1907 Count Giulio Guicciardini Corsi Salviati got rid of the conservatories and restored parterres and formal flower gardens. A labyrinth and green theatre were introduced in the eastern part of the garden. The *claire-voyée*, the fishponds, and the *ragnaia* for bird hunting still survive. In the *ragnaia* a long runnel, used as a drinking trough, is in an avenue of holm oaks, now partly excluded from the garden and used as a public park.

The lemon garden at Corsi Salviati, surrounding the circular pond, dates to the 18th century.

Florence: Villa Medici at Fiesole

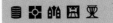

Location: via Mantellini, Fiesole. 8km (5 miles) N of Florence

open: By appointment only, daily, every morning except Sat and Sun

Further information from:
Via Mantellini, Fiesole, Florence
Tel: 055 59164 and 59417

Nearby sights of interest:
Fiesole, including cathedral, church of Sant'Alessandro, Roman theatre, San Domenico di Fiesole, monastery of San Francesco, and outstanding view of city of Florence.

The Villa Medici at Fiesole has a breathtaking view of Florence and the valley of Arno. It was built between 1450–57 for Giovanni de' Medici. The construction of the palace involved great expenditure on the gigantic walls that support the terraces – intended to resemble the Hanging Gardens of Babylon. The upper terrace was devoted to rare flowers and herbs, while the lower one was used as kitchen garden. The warmth provided by the walls also enabled the cultivatation of espaliered citrus. We know that Giovanni grew *Rosa* x *alba* 'Incarnata', now known as 'Maiden's Blush', and many varieties of dianthus. The property was inherited by Lorenzo de Medici, "il Magnifico", who made the villa a cultural centre during the Renaissance. Changes made from about 1760 by Lady Elisabeth Walpole included some Baroque decoration and a new coach avenue. In the 19th century William Blundell Spence altered the garden to satisfy Victorian taste, and conservatories were built on the lower and upper terrace. The garden and the building were restored in the second decade of 20th century by the English architect Cecil Pinsent. He designed simple box parterres on the lower and west terraces, in order to give the garden a Renaissance atmosphere.

The lower garden with box-edged beds designed by Cecil Pinsent are a 20th-century addition to the 15th-century Villa Medici.

open: All year, except the second and third Mon of each month, daily 9am–variable depending on season

open: Guided tours only

Further information from:
Via della Petraia, 50141 Firenze
Tel: 055 452691
Fax: 055 219397

Nearby sights of interest:
Villa Medicea di Castello (access with same ticket); Villa Guicciardini Corsi Salviati at Sesto Fiorentino.

13 *Florence: Villa della Petraia*

Location: Castello, 6km (3¾ miles) NW of Florence

Transformed into a Renaissance villa in 1537 by the Duke Cosimo I de' Medici, from a medieval castle, the gardens of La Petraia are contemporary with those of the neighbouring Villa di Castello. Work proceeded very slowly until 1587 when Ferdinando, the second son of Cosimo I, became Grand Duke of Tuscany. He hired the architect Raffaello Pagni, who laid out the grounds in three terraces: the upper terrace, later named Piano della Figurina (Terrace of the Little Statue), the middle terrace, the *giardino segreto*, and the lower terrace which became a *frutteto* (orchard). The latter had an unusual shape of two tangent circles inscribed in a rectangle. The garden is illustrated in one of Utens' lunettes in the Topographical Museum in Florence. In 1872, when the villa became the property of the King Vittorio Emmanuele II of Savoy, the garden was divided into small beds for bedding-out displays and the original shape was transformed into an ellipse.

The whole garden has been recently replanted with historic collections in order to recall both the 16th-century Medici and the 19th-century Savoy taste in flowers. The northern sections of the lower garden have been stocked with dwarf fruit trees,

Planting at the Medici villa of Petraia has been restored to respect both 16th-century and 19th-century tastes.

popular features in Medici gardens, while masses of irises, roses and annuals recall the gardening style of the late 19th century. In the middle terrace a large fishpond, built in about 1590, still collects the water provided by the Medici aqueduct for the irrigation of the garden. The western section of the terrace, originally the *giardino segreto*, is planted for springtime with a collection of old, now rare, varieties of bulbs. The upper terrace became the most altered when in 1872, Emmanuele di Mirafiore, the illegitimate son of the King Vittorio Emmanuele II, married Blanche de Larderel and a great ball was given to celebrate their engagement. The simple Renaissance compartments of the eastern terrace were transformed into curvilinear shapes around the Fountain of Fiorenza by Tribolo, Pierino da Vinci and Giambologna. Here the 19th-century planting scheme has recently been reinstated.

Florence: Villa La Pietra

Location: 1.5km (1 mile) N of Florence

Originally built in 1462, this capacious Tuscan mansion is now surrounded by an extensive Renaissance revival garden from which one can gain delightful framed prospects to Florence.

The villa was recast in the 16th century and the formal gardens were replaced in the early 19th century by a *giardino inglese*. The present grounds were laid out around 1908–10 for Arthur Acton by the French garden designer Henri Duchêne, father of Achille. The gardens were subsequently "restored" in about 1915 by Diego Suarez. Arthur's son, Sir Harold, also made various changes, including relocating garden buildings and sculptures.

These theatrical gardens, which are a bold Anglo-American interpretation of an Italian Renaissance garden, are divided into a series of rooms described by high bay and box hedges staged over a series of "depending" terraces linked by steps and paths.

The terraces are criss-crossed by box hedges, grass *allées* and glades, many of which are dotted with bay and cypress sentinels dwarfed by holm oaks, and stately pines. Venetian marble statuary, "ruined" triumphal arches and pergolas terminate vistas, line paths and frame views to the rolling countryside beyond. The 17th-century *pomario* (walled orchard) is encircled by *rocaille*-encrusted walls which enclose a sprawling *stanzone* (orangery), a Baroque pool, vines, fruit trees and clipped evergreens.

The estate was bequeathed by Sir Harold to New York University and the villa now serves as a centre for Italian studies.

open: By appointment only (New York University)
open: As above

Further information from:
120 Via Bolognese, Florence
Fax: 055 472 725

Nearby sights of interest:
Florence; Villa Pratolino and Giambologna statue of the Apennines further along the Via Bolognese.

At La Pietra the green theatre has box balls as footlights and "wings" of yew.

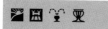

open: Sun only
open: As above

Further information from:
Via Bolognese, Vaglia, Florence
Tel: 055 2760529 and 2760538

Nearby sights of interest:
Florence, including Villa La Pietra
and nearby Giambologna statue.

Buontalenti's chapel is one of the
remaining original buildings.

15 *Florence: Villa Pratolino (Parco Demidoff)*

Location: Pratolino, 12km (7½ miles) N of Florence on the old road to Bologna

This large landscape park preserves little of the extraordinary garden created by Buontalenti for Francesco I de' Medici from 1569. Statues, grottoes, fountains, and water jokes were once displayed in the formal park to the north and the south.

Pratolino was famous during the late Renaissance and many of its features were copied and incorporated in gardens in northern Europe such as the Palatine Gardens in Germany and Wilton House in England. The villa, neglected during the 18th century, was destroyed in 1821, and a few years later the grounds were transformed into an English landscape park by the Bohemian gardener, Joseph Frietsch. The wealthy Russian Demidoff family acquired the park in 1872.

A few remarkable features of the original garden have been restored, including the *Appennino*, the giant sculpture designed by Giambologna, standing at the head of the lake in the north area of the garden, the Gamberaie – a series of pools on different levels used for crayfish – and the Grotto of Cupid, which has interior walls covered with tufa and stalactites.

open: By appointment, Mon, Wed, Fri 9am–12pm

Further information from:
Botanical Garden of Florence
Via Micheli 3, 50121 Florence
Tel: 055 2757402
Fax: 055 2757438

Nearby sights of interest:
Florence, including church of San Marco, museums of Beato Angelico and the Uffizi, Boboli Garden, Villa Capponi, Giardino dei Semplici, churches of Santo Spirito and Santa Felicita, Ponte Vecchio, and monuments of the Piazza del Duomo.

16 *Florence: Giardino dei Semplici*

Location: Via Micheli in the centre of the city

The Giardino dei Semplici was created by order of Cosimo I de' Medici in 1545. *Semplici* (simples) in the 16th century were those parts of plants considered capable of therapeutic power. The original layout was by Tribolo. In 1718 the garden was restored and the collections were improved. Today only the entrance gate from Via La Pira and the central fountain remain from the 16th-century layout. The garden is organized into 20 main beds with a few minor beds for perennials. Among the most remarkable specimens a horse chestnut, *Aesculus hippocastanum*, a *Zelkova serrata*, a 200-year-old cork oak *(Quercus suber)*, and *Washingtonia filifera*, are all worthy of note. In the cold conservatories there is a large collection of Cycadaceae. In the hot houses "useful" plants, such as *Cyperus papyrus, Musa sapientium, Theobroma cacao*, black palm *(Astrocaryum mexicanum)*, and the breadfruit tree *(Artocarpus altilis)* are displayed.

Villa i Tatti

Location: Settignano, 8km (5 miles) NE of Florence

open: By appointment only
(University of Harvard)
open: As above

Further information from:
Via di Vincigliata 26,
50014 Fiesole
Tel: 055 603251

Nearby sights of interest:
Villa Gamberaia at Settignano;
the city of Florence.

The Villa i Tatti was lived in by the famous art historian Bernard Berenson from 1900 until his death in 1959. The young British architect Cecil Pinsent was engaged by Berenson's wife, Mary Pearsall Smith, to transform the garden, with advice from the architectural historian Geoffrey Scott, author of the essay "Architecture of Humanism".

The garden, started in 1911 and finished in 1916, is one of the first examples of the revival of the Italian Renaissance garden style, particularly appreciated by the conspicuous Anglo-American community that settled in the hills around Florence at the beginning of this century. The architectural decoration is mostly derived from the repertory of the Mannerist and Baroque style in Tuscan gardens.

The main garden or Green Garden, laid out down the gentle slope beyond the *limonaia* in front of the villa, is arranged in geometric parterres framed by box hedges and pyramids on both sides of a central path paved with pebble mosaic. At the bottom of the main garden two balustraded stairs lead down into the *boschetto*, planted with holm oaks according to the Tuscan tradition. From here a turf avenue edged by cypresses leads back to the eastern terrace of the villa, where there is the old chapel in which Bernard and Mary Berenson are buried.

The garden was conceived as an architectural space dominated by geometrically clipped evergreens in which flowers have no place. At this time it was still believed that the original Renaissance gardens had no flowers. At Villa i Tatti the only place for flowers is in the secret garden between the house, the *limonaia* and the west terrace garden.

Other parts of the grounds, including the wilderness and the gazebo, were not designed by Pinsent or Scott but by an unknown architect. The villa now belongs to Harvard University and has become a prestigious institute for Renaissance art studies.

At Villa i Tatti Cecil Pinsent designed the garden for Bernard Berenson and his wife. The Renaissance-style Green Garden lies on a slope beneath the house.

open: By appointment only, Wed 1pm–5pm

Further information from:
53042 Chianciano Terme, Siena
Tel: 0578 69101

Nearby sights of interest:
Spa town of Chianciano Terme;
hill-town of Montepulciano;
Renaissance town of Pienza;
village of San Quírico d'Orcia.

18 *Villa La Foce*

Location: SW of Chianciano Terme, 8km (5 miles) from Montepulciano

La Foce is a green oasis in the barren Siena countryside, with elegant walled enclosures, soaring cypress walks, native cyclamen and box-edged beds, flowerbeds, lawns, and wild flower meadows.

The garden was the inspiration of Iris Origo, the writer and horticulturalist, who between 1927–39 employed the British architect Cecil Pinsent to restore the villa and create a "new" garden in Renaissance style. From the first garden, in front of the house, planted with box hedges surrounding a fountain, a gate leads to the main garden. This is a large terrace divided into compartments by clipped box hedges around turfed enclosures. A garden room under a pergola is draped with wisteria with mats of aubretia and alyssum scrambling over the low stone walls. At the bottom a terrace looks down on a formal sunken garden, with box hedges, two *Magnolia grandiflora*, and cypress trees framing views out to the countryside. It is reached by stairways on both sides of a grotto carved in the local stone. The pergola on the upper terrace is also clothed with *Wisteria sinensis*, with twining roses and beds of bush roses on its upper side. The pergola finally reaches a terrace from which there is a breathtaking view.

The walk continues up into the wild garden, planted with pomegranates and Judas trees *(Cercis siliquastrum)*, the latter's flowers echoing the purple blooms of the wisteria on the pergola, and white-flowered spireas surrounded by wild flowers. From the end of the garden a path leads to a chapel and graveyard, designed by Pinsent in a pure Renaissance style.

The last part of the garden at La Foce to be completed. Pinsent's design is a geometric garden with cypresses framing the view.

Lucca: *Villa Garzoni*

Location: Callodi, 17km (11 miles) NE of Lucca, off S 435

open: Daily, 1 Feb to 30 Nov, 9am to sunset

Villa Garzoni, perhaps the most magnificent of a chain of villas that stud the hills north-east of Lucca, proudly surveys the village of Collodi, which scrambles untidily down the hillside behind. The garden has been described as "more lordly park than intimate garden", and constitutes "despite its gross details, one of the triumphs of garden design and planning of the 17th century". Ideally the visitor should descend through a *bosco* of holm oak, cypress, bay and box to the head of the cascade. Unfortunately, the majestic effect of this is presently diminished by restoration works. Hopefully we shall soon see "the steps and glimpse of the parterre, the pools with their gigantic sprays flung forty feet into the air, the dancing hedges, and then away beyond the rich open country". As we descend along the edge of the cascade the gardens open out before us, and when we reach the highest of the three terraces we can "feast upon the wealth of the parterre below". Despite the restoration the gardens have an air of shabbiness, particularly the Boschetto dei Bambu and the virtually vanished maze. For three centuries Garzoni has inspired poetry and prose, including Abarra's *"Le pompe di collodi"* (1652).

Further information from:
Via di Castello, 51014 Collodi (PT)
Tel: 0572 429131 and 429116

Nearby sights of interest:
Villa Mansi; Villa Reale; Villa Torrigiani; city of Lucca.

Part of the recently restored Baroque parterre at Villa Garzoni.

Lucca: *Villa Mansi*

Location: Segromigno in Monte, 12km (8 miles) NE of Lucca

open: All year, daily except Mon, 9am–7pm, Sun 9am–2pm
open: As above

Villa Mansi stands out among its rival Lucchese palaces on account of its handsome villa and the evocative remains of its once elaborate water gardens, designed by the late Baroque architect, Filippo Juvarra. The present house, begun in the late 16th century, was rebuilt in the 1630s, but was then recast for the Mansi family in the 1670s. It was not until the 1720s that the early gardens were altered by Juvarra and given the theatrical stamp that they bear to this day. At Villa Mansi his legacy reminds us of the bold stage designs that he produced for Cardinal Ottoboni's theatre in Cancelleria: cunning perspectives were contrived by a network of tall evergreen hedges and pools, cascades and fountains, forming spectacular *termini* and incidents throughout the gardens. Of the many conceits known to have been erected to the master's designs only the fishpond, the ruins of Diana's grotto, a section of a cascade, and segments of hedges survive. In the 19th century the formal east gardens, and much of what survived of Juvarra's garden were swept away in favour of a *giardino inglese*. This informal landscape is not, however,

Further information from:
Via Galli Tassi, 55100 Lucca (LU)
Tel: 0583 55570

Nearby sights of interest:
Villa Reale; Villa Garzoni; Villa Torrigiani; city of Lucca, including the old town, cathedral of San Martino, and church of San Michele.

merit and reflects the aristocratic Lucchese obsession with botanical fashion. The stately exotic forest trees include *Pseudotsuga menziesii*, *Picea abies*, *Chamaecyparis lawsoniana*, and *Cedrus libani* ssp. *atlantica*, mixed with native *Quercus petraea* and *Quercus ilex*. A ring of nine majestic *Liriodendron tulipifera* forms a remarkable eye-catcher upon the spacious lawn. A bamboo grove (*Phyllostachys nigra*) and small forlorn Japanese banana plantation (*Musa basjoo*) bestow an air of exoticism of which, were they still in residence, the Mansi might well approve.

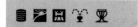

open: 1 Mar to 30 Nov, daily except Mon; guided tours at 10am–11am, 3pm–6pm on the hour

Further information from:
Via Villa Reale, 55014 Marlia (LU)
Tel: 0538 30108 and 30009

Nearby sights of interest:
Villa Garzoni, Villa Mansi; Villa Torrigiani; Lucca, including the old town, cathedral, and church of San Michele.

This Baroque garden is one of the most beautiful in Italy.

Lucca: Villa Reale, Marlia

Location: 8 km (5 miles) NE of Lucca

The Villa Marlia lies at the heart of one of Tuscany's most grandiose noble estates, nestled in the Pizzorne hills northeast of Lucca at the source of the River Serchio, which flows to the sea at Viareggio. The villa, built by the Orsetti (*c.*1651), was originally known as Villa Marilla – its name being changed by Stefano Orsetti in honour of Louis XIV's château at Marly. The villa was subsequently recast by its owners, the most celebrated of whom was Elisa Baciocchi – Napoleon Bonaparte's sister.

Finding the estate rather too small, this tireless improver turned out her neighbour the Bishop of Lucca at Vescovato, and bought up her neighbours' farms and fields to assemble a demesne befitting her status. The commission to remodel the lot was given to Morel, who had worked for Empress Josephine at Malmaison. The palace sits atop a broad lawn which sweeps

down through the *parco* to a huge pool. On either side of this emerald piste are clumps and woods of *Cedrus libani* ssp. *atlantica, Fagus sylvatica, Ginkgo biloba, Liriodendron tulipifera, Pinus nigra, Pinus strobus,* and evergreen oaks.

Fortunately, the arrival of the British in 1814 ensured that much of the 17th-century gardens of the Villa Marlia survives: we can still see the extraordinary Baroque green amphitheatre of sculpted yew and box (where Paganini often performed for Baciocchi); the large semicircular fountain behind the villa, infested with statues of Jupiter, Saturn, Adonis, and Pomona on a topiary stage pierced by a giant cascade; the Palazzina dell'Orologio; the Grotto of Pan; and the long fishpond crowned with a semi-circular *nymphaeum*, where heroic recumbent statues of the river gods Arno and the Serchio pour copious streams of water to feed the pool. The gardens were recently restored by the present proprietor, Countess Pecci Blunt, who bought the estate in 1923.

22 *Lucca: Villa Massei*

Location: 13 km (8 miles) SE of Lucca, SS 439 near Compitese Hills

A series of intimate formal garden compartments laid out since 1982, when the property was acquired by Gil Cohen and Paul Gervais from Boston, surround the main house, a 16th–century hunting lodge, where tall cypresses and silvery olives complement the ancient retaining walls, a pair of 300-year-old cypresses framing a view to the Apian Alps across the valley of the Serchio at Lucca. The garden with its box-edged beds on the terrace gives a hint of historical authenticity but planting in them of outrageous "hot" coloured flowers gives a thoroughly modern twist. Sun-loving helianthus, Mexican tithonias, marvels of Peru *(Mirabilis jalapa)* and Indian shot (forms of canna) are the main ingredients – both of the latter plants from the New World were known and grown in the 16th-century Medici gardens in Florence – all enjoying the Tuscan summer heat. A parterre of alpine strawberries flanks an open loggia, taking its inspiration from medieval monastery gardens in which plants with medicinal or culinary uses were planted in easy-to-maintain geometrically shaped beds. Water flows from a Renaissance *nymphaeum* to disappear underground and reappear in a dolphin niche below.

A camphor tree *(Cinnamomum camphora)* with deliciously scented leaves was planted in the 19th century and is now 15m (50ft) high. A *viale* of cherries, *Prunus* 'Reine de Marche', leads through a meadow of wild flowers to distant olive groves.

open: May to Sept by appointment via fax

open: As above

Further information from:
55060 Massa Macinaia, Lucca
Fax: 0583 90138

Nearby sights of interest:
Lucca, including the old town, cathedral, and church of San Michele.

New World plants such as marvels of Peru were introduced in the 16th century.

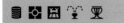

open: 1 Mar–31 Oct, daily except Tue, 10am–12pm, 3pm to sunset
open: As above

Further information from:
Camigliano (LU)
Tel: 0583 928008

Nearby sights of interest:
Villa Reale, Villa Mansi, Villa Garzoni, Lucca, including the old town, cathedral of San Martino, church of San Michele.

A view from a staircase that overlooks the Giardino di Flora at the Villa Torrigiani.

23 *Lucca: Villa Torrigiani*

Location: 12km (7½ miles) NE of Lucca, take Florence sea motorway, exit Capannori

Villa Torrigiani is also known as Villa di Camigliano – named after the camellia that was introduced to the gardens in the early 18th century. The gardens were originally laid out in the Italian Renaissance style, and subsequently remodelled in the 17th century by the Marchese Nicolao Santini, Ambassador from the Republic of Lucca to the court of Louis XIV. The present Baroque layout, arranged on two levels, may be by André Le Nôtre. The celebrated French landscape gardener was apparently invited to redesign the setting after having presented plans of Versailles to Pope Urban VIII, presumably in the presence of Santini. All that survives of Le Nôtre's work is the symmetrical reflecting pools in front of the villa; the extensive *parco* north of the villa has been lost, although ruins of an eye-catcher can be discerned in the distance.

Those who wish to study the layout of the garden as it appeared in the late 18th century are recommended to examine the survey of the grounds prepared by Jacopo Farnocchia that hangs in the villa. The most outstanding part of the garden is the secret garden or Giardino di Flora, laid out with its regular beds, topiary and pools. The whole garden, including the large *pietra spugnosa* encrusted *ninfeo*, is riddled with concealed *scherzosi giochi d'acqua* that erupt from statuary, steps, and masks, as well as from the ground amidst the pebbles. Various impressive trees planted in the 19th century include *Libocedrus decurrens*, *Taxodium distichum*, *Sequoia sempervirens*, and *Ginkgo biloba*, as well as magnificent evergeen magnolias, cypresses and umbrella pines. The 18th-century avenue of cypresses that leads to the villa from the village of Borgonuova is remarkable and unique, a fine reminder of the past grandeur of not only this but neighbouring estates in the region.

Villa Caprile

Location: from Pesaro, follow signs to Rimini on SS 16

This typical Marche villa, built amidst the *vigne* of the Pesaro countryside, was between 1817–18 the home of Caroline of Brunswick, wife of the Prince Regent (and future George IV), when she was carrying on with Bartolomeo Pergami. The villa was built around 1640 and was altered several times over the following centuries. Its tiered garden layout was contrived to respond to the landscape around the town of Pesaro, which is made up of rolling hills, terraced as vineyards, interspersed with clumps of trees. The layout of the villa garden consists of three terraces, one of which is a sheltered garden room, protected from the sea breezes by the bulk of the house. The gardens have a range of 17th-century *scherzi d'acqua* which, concealed amidst the garden stairs and seats, conspire to shower the unwary. The water games were recently restored and have become the foremost attraction at the gardens, drawing great numbers of visitors seeking respite from the summer heat. A less visited spot is the shady *bosco* that lies at a distance from the house. The gardens were extended in 1780 at which time a now vanished green theatre was inserted in the *bosco*. The gardens are maintained by its present owners, the Agricultural Institute of Pesaro.

open: 1 Jul to 15 Sep, 3pm–7pm, and by appointment through Istituto Tecnico Agrario A. Cecchi (0721 21440)
open: As above

Further information from:
Via Caprile 1, 61100 Pesaro
Tel: 0721 21418 and 21440
Fax: 0721 21418

Nearby sights of interest:
Town of Pesaro, including Museo Civici and Palazzo Ducale.

At the Villa Caprile the early layout and 17th-century water jokes are still maintained.

open: Jun to Sep; contact
Azienda di Soggiorno of Pesaro
(Tel 0721 69341) or the local Town
Council
open: As above

Further information from:
Via S. Bartolo 63, 61100 Pesaro
Tel: 0721 23603

Nearby sights of interest:
Pesaro, including Villa Imperiale,
Museo Civici, and Palazzo Ducale.

**The garden at the Villa Imperiale
is terraced on three levels in
typical Renaissance style.**

25 *Pesaro: Villa Imperiale*

Location: 2km (1¼ miles) NW of Pesaro

This spectacular Renaissance summer palace lies west of Pesaro,
perched on the steep slope of Mount San Bartolo. The site was
chosen by Alessandro Sforza, who built his palace between
1469–72. It was subsequently enlarged by Girolamo Genga, who
in 1530 was commissioned to transform the semi-fortified country
house into a Renaissance villa. Given Genga's acquaintance with
Raphael's work, it is not surprising to find that Imperiale owes
much, both in terms of the architecture and the garden design,
to the Villa Farnesina Chigi (p.113) and Villa Madama in Rome.

The garden was "typically Renaissance", not only because
of its enclosed axial plan and layout, but because of the planting:
largely evergreen and including myrtles, bays, vines, and citrus
trees. The walls of the lower gardens were covered with espaliers
of bitter oranges, and lemon hybrids, known as *bizzarie*, were
grown in parterres. The palace interior still has an exquisite
trompe l'oeil painting that depicts the plants for which the
garden was famous. Among the many remarkable features of
the garden are the *sala scoverta*, surrounded by grottoes, porticos
and shell-encrusted rooms with fountains. One of the greatest
achievements was the introduction of water, acquired with great
skill and at vast expense. The garden later began a long period of
decline and sustained serious damage during World War II. It has
now been restored by Count Guglielmo Castelbarco Albani.

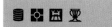

open: 1 Jun to 15 Sep, daily,
3–7pm, and by appointment
through Istituto Tecnico Agrario A.
Cecchi (0721 21440)
open: As above

Further information from:
Via Miralfiore, 61100 Pesaro
Tel 0721 21418 and 21440
Fax 0721 21418

Nearby sights of interest:
Town of Pesaro, including Villa
Imperiale, Museo Civici, and
Palazzo Ducale.

26 *Pesaro: Villa Miralfiore*

Location: Via Miralfiore in the centre of the town

The Villa Miralfiore, unlike the neighbouring Villa Imperiale,
stands on a level site not far from the old walls of Pesaro. The
villa was rebuilt in about 1559 for Duke Guidobalso II, son of
Francesco Maria della Rovere, to the designs of Girolamo
Genga's son Bartolomeo, and was subsequently redesigned in
the mid 17th century by Carlo Emmanuele I, who is said to
have sought the advice of Bernini and Borromini. The villa has
always been well kept, and the garden is laid out in three very
fine parterres laid out in the most robust simplicity. These
gardens, mostly outlined in box, are purported to preserve their
original late 16th-century layout. A range of greenhouses and
a neo-classical colonnade stand at the end of the parterres behind
the house, which separate them from the *bosco*. The brick walls
which enclose the gardens are particularly attractive.

27 *Pienza: Palazzo Piccolomini*

Location: 50km (31 miles) SE of Siena, E of S 2

Pienza still retains the architectural shape and urban plan created for Pope Pio II in 1485. His classic and humanistic education made him transfom the medieval village of Corsignano, where he was born, into a town that accorded to the Renaissance ideals of proportion and symmetry. A trapezoidal square, with the cathedral on the south side and two palaces on either side, became the focal point of the plan. The Palazzo Piccolomini on the west side of the square was designed by Rossellino. Its garden side has loggias on three stories facing the garden to the south and a vast view of the Val d'Orcia, Monte Amiata, and the fortress of Radocofani on the old road to Rome. The garden is built on a terrace and is probably a simpler version of the gardens of Villa Medici in Fiesole (p.75). The garden, unlike the terraces at Fiesole which are open to the landscape, are enclosed by a wall with three arched openings framing the landscape. The enclosure makes the garden seem like an open-air room and thus a continuation of the house, creating a link with the landscape. In the 1930s the garden was "restored". Four compartments were laid out framed with box hedges, more suitable to a Victorian garden, and clipped bay trees were planted at each corner, according to the fashionable Italian garden revival taste.

open: Daily, except Mon and public holidays 10–12.30am, 3–6pm winter, 10–12.30am, 4–7pm summer; closed 20 Nov–7 Dec and 26 Feb–8 Mar
open: As above

Further information from:
Piazza Pio II, 53026 Pienza (SI)
Tel: 0578 284300 and 748 503

Nearby sights of interest:
Pienza, including the cathedral and the Museo; city of Siena.

Although the restoration of the garden of the Palazzo Piccolomini is not authentic, the clipped bays in box-edged beds have a Renaissance resonance.

28 *Pisa: Orto Botanico*

Location: Via Luca Ghini, within walking distance of the cathedral in N of the city

open: All year, daily except Sun and public holidays, Mon to Fri 8am –1pm, 2pm–5pm, Sat 8am–1pm

Further information from:
Via Luca Ghini 5, 56126 Pisa
Tel: 050 560045
Fax: 050 55135

Nearby sights of interest:
City of Pisa, including Piazza del Duomo with the cathedral, Campo Santo, and the Leaning Tower, Museo Nazionale, and Piazza dei Cavalieri.

At the Orto Botanico in Pisa there is a fine collection of plants suitable for the relatively mild climate.

The botanic garden of the University of Pisa was founded by the Duke of Tuscany, Cosimo I, in 1544 and is, together with Padua, the oldest botanical garden in Europe. The first curator was the naturalist Luca Ghini. After having been moved twice, the garden was established on this site and completed in 1595 by the Flemish botanist Joseph Goedenhuitze (known as Casabona).

It was laid out in eight square compartments in which the beds had a very complex pattern. The plants were mainly chosen for their medical properties with their parts used for the preparation of medicine in the nearby *Fonderia*. Attached to the garden was the *Galleria*, where natural items, exotic objects and portraits of famous naturalists were shown.

The original layout was preserved until the mid 18th century, when the two southern compartments were obliterated by the enlargment of the Museum of Natural History. The garden was extended to the east in 1841, while the northern sides were enlarged in about 1900, with a new arboretum. The original beds were dismantled and replaced with narrow rectilinear beds, in order to update the garden to modern criteria of botanical classification. Nevertheless, six surviving compartments with central fountains still reflect the original layout.

29 *Certosa di Pontignano*

Location: Pontignano, 10km (6¼ miles) from Siena on SS 326

The monastery of Pontignano was founded in 1343 and enlarged in the following century. In 1784 it was sold to the hermits of Monte Celso and then to the noble family Sergardi, who used it as countryside villa. Today it belongs to the University of Siena. An 18th-century engraving shows the gardens at a lower level below the two vast cloisters. A double stair descended from a loggia to the main garden, divided into three main compartments, further subdivided into square beds. At the centre there was a *peschiera* (reservoir) with a large orchard on the east. The garden still preserves the outlines of this original layout and the central *peschiera*, protected by an iron fence. A large *ragnaia* – originally a wood for hunting birds – screens the garden along the north side.

Tall hedges of holm oaks, perfectly clipped on their vertical sides and horizontal top, frame a rectangular space. This type of clipping in the Siena area was done to stretch the nets for the hunting of birds and it testifies to the high standard of gardening technique in early Tuscan traditions. The *ragnaia* is one of the few in Tuscany that has maintained its traditional geometric clipped appearance. The garden has a beautiful collection of citrus and a colourful flower display during the summer.

open: Daily by appointment
open: As above

Further information from:
Pontignano, 53010 Castelnuovo
Berardenga, Siena
Tel: 0577 356851
Fax: 0577 356669

Nearby sights of interest:
Siena, including cathedral and
Piazza del Campo; Villa La Foce.

**At Pontignano the garden lies
below the 14th-century cloisters.**

30 *Venzano*

Location: 13km (8 miles) from Volterra, the last three miles a rough track

This is a new garden and a nursery for herbs and perennials on the site of an old Augustinian monastery. Two Australians are simultaneously creating a pleasure garden and providing plants for local gardeners. Old olive and vine terraces are being replanted not only with traditional "crops" but with varieties of plants chosen chiefly for their aromatic attractions and suitability in the sharp cold winters and hot dry summers of Tuscany. Tender roses such as 'Cooper's Burmese' survive against the house walls. They have inherited some old *Zizyphus jujuba* trees, as well as venerable pomegranates, while bay hedges now define and enclose *giardini segreti* near the house, extending the architecture. Paths and steps lead to a Roman spring and to terraces and sloping banks clothed with a mixture of Mediterranean roses, rosemaries, lavender, cistus, phlomis, pinks, creeping thymes, and romneyas. Pots contain rarer treasures, including jasmines, lilies, hedychiums, salvias, South African bulbs, and pelargoniums with scented leaves.

open: Thurs, Fri, Sat
9am–1pm, 2pm–6pm

Further information from:
Loc. Venzano, Mazzolla, 56048
Volterra (PI)
Tel: 0588 39095 Don Leevers

Nearby sights of interest:
Town of Volterra, including Piazza
dei Priori, cathedral, Battistero,
Porta all' Arco, and Museo Etrusco
Guarnacci.

Key to gardens

1 Villa Adriana
2 Villa Aldobrandini
3 Isola Bisentina
4 Villa Lante
5 Bomarzo: Sacro Bosco
6 Villa Farnese
7 Villa d'Este

8 Castel Gandolfo
9 Giardini della Landriana
10 San Liberato
11 Giardino di Ninfa
12 Villa Borghese
13 Villa Celimontana
14 Orto Botanico, Rome

15 Villa Doria Pamphili
16 Villa Farnesina
17 Orti Farnesiani
18 Villa Giulia
19 Villa Medici
20 Vatican Gardens
21 Castello Ruspoli

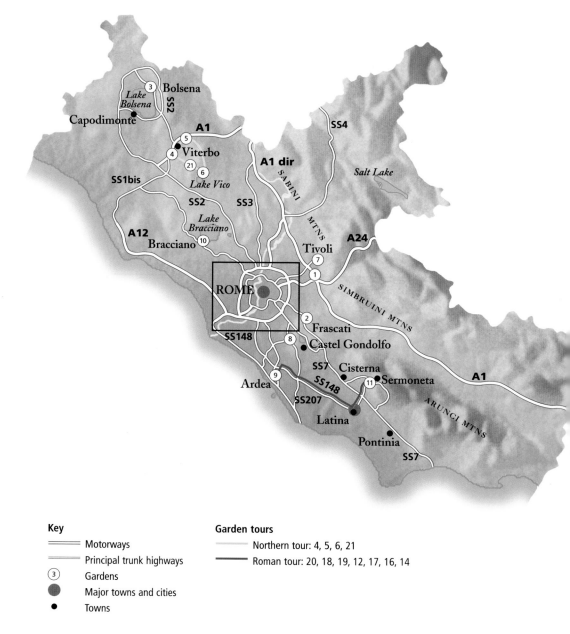

Key

Motorways

Principal trunk highways

(3) Gardens

Major towns and cities

• Towns

Garden tours

Northern tour: 4, 5, 6, 21

Roman tour: 20, 18, 19, 12, 17, 16, 14

Rome & its Environs

In Rome, towards the end of the 15th and the start of the 16th centuries, architects such as Donato Bramante (1444-1514), abandoned the medieval conception of the garden as a *hortus conclusus* to place a new emphasis on a severely architectural approach to design, mixed with the development of the humanist ideals of country life in which agriculture and intellectual pursuits were all part of "living", with the garden as a link between the countryside and the villa. Bramante used concepts emulating classical Roman models, having measured and studied the ruins of the Emperor Hadrian's villa at Tivoli and the Temple of Fortune of Praeneste at Palestrina. His plan for the Cortile del Belvedere for Pope Julius II, begun in 1503, was revolutionary. Bramante related current trends in the study of perspective in painting to garden building, moulding the terrain with a series of terraces, linked by monumental steps and ramps, dominated by a central perspective that traversed the terraces at right angles to culminate in a final semicircular niche. The principles of symmetry and proportion were further developed in and around

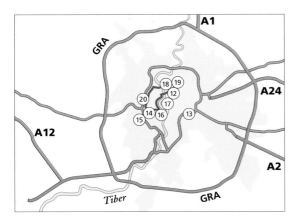

A map showing the gardens to be found in the city centre of Rome.

Rome by Raphael (1483–1520), particularly at the Villa Madama (now seldom accessible), and Baldassare Peruzzi (1481–1537), who also worked in Siena, Giacomo Barozzi da Vignola (1505–73), and Pirro Ligorio (c.1500–83) to include ever more dramatic terracing, water cascades and *giochi d'acqua*, distorting perspectives and visually extending the garden into the countryside in a more Baroque style. Many of the greatest gardens in or near Rome that date from the second half of the 16th century – the Villa Lante at Bagnaia, (pp.96–99), Palazzo Farnese at Caprarola (p.101), and Villa d'Este at Tivoli (p.102), and the 17th-century villas at Frascati – take advantage of dramatic hillside sites to exploit the use of terracing and theatrical water displays.

The climate of Rome is less extreme than that of Florence but except for relatively recently planted gardens, such as those of Ninfa in the once-malarial plains south of Rome (pp.106–109), and Landriana at Anzio (p.104), plants have never been of primary importance in the development of garden design, although individuals such as Francesco Caetani were important collectors of new rarities in the early 16th century. The most important early botanical collection was made in the Horti Farnesiani (p.113), a garden laid out with aviaries by Vignola for Pope Paul III in 1534–39. The catalogue of plants grown there in 1625 is an important source for establishing which plants were grown in Rome in the early 17th century. Falda's etchings of the *Gardens of Rome* (1683) trace contemporary styles and show how often French-style parterres of curvilinear scrollwork have replaced the earlier more geometrical layouts typical of Renaissance gardens. Today, visitors can still appreciate the architectural gardens that have strongly influenced the development of garden design throughout the western world.

At La Landriana outside Rome arum lilies *(Zantedeschia aethiopica)* flower luxuriantly beside the lake.

Villa Adriana, Tivoli

Location: 31km (19 miles) E of Rome on S 5

Villa Adriana (Hadrian's Villa) at Tivoli is one of the greatest monuments of antiquity, and enough remains of the buildings and layout to interest both architects and gardeners. A whole city rather than just a dwelling, it was built by Adrian (Publius Aelius Hadrianus) after he became emperor in AD 117. It is extremely extensive and complex and many of the architectural features were a source of inspiration for architects during the Renaissance. Particularly remarkable was the hydraulic system that fed water to the main structures. Fountains, pools, reservoirs, and canals connect the various buildings throughout.

Today the site is still magical with wild flowers growing in the hay meadows, tall cypresses and enough of the remaining features to make it well worth exploring. Among these are the fishpond in the Pecile area, and the Canopus, a long pool which was meant to recall the canal that led from Alexandria to Canopus, a town on the Nile delta. At its northern end there are the ruins of a *triclinium*, used for dinners. Another important feature is the Maritime Theatre, a circular pond framed by Ionic columns that encircles a small island, where a *domus* (miniature palace) was built. For their technical accomplishment the Great Therms, or baths, are remarkable.

Villa Aldobrandini, Frascati

Location: Frascati, 22km (13½ miles) from Rome

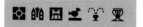

The Villa Aldobrandini is the largest and the most spectacular of the late Renaissance villas built in Frascati. Cardinal Pietro Aldobrandini was given the villa by his uncle Pope Clemente VII in 1598. Behind the palace a vast courtyard, the Water Theatre, is framed by a wall ornamented with Ionic pilasters and niches. The central niche contains the Fountain of Atlas. In the side niches are sculptures of Polyphemus playing the pipes and the Centaur playing the horn. Subterranean rooms in the base of the *nymphaeum* are shaded by the palace. A chamber on the left is dedicated to San Sebastian and one on the right is known as the "Room of the Winds". On the terrace behind the Atlas the great runnel of water, which flows from the top of the hill over a *scala d'acqua*, is enclosed by an alley of clipped holm oaks. This leads to a pair of columns of Hercules. In the wood on the top of the hill a small grotto entrance, carved by Mida in 1612 as a monstrous face, recalls the more famous monsters of Bomarzo (p.100).

Isola Bisentina

Location: 30km (18½ miles) NW of Viterbo, Via Cassia north, direction Capodimonte; ferry service from Bolsena or Capodimonte

open: By previous appointment with one of the ferry companies 1 Apr to 31 Oct

This small island has been inhabited almost continuously since the Bronze Age and is outstandingly rich in both architectural and horticultural art. In 1516 the future Pope Paul III, built two temples one of which, La Rocchina, is still well preserved. From the early 16th century the island served as a hunting and fishing estate for Pope Leo X. During successive changes of ownership the island and its buildings drifted slowly into decline until its purchase in 1912 by the Principessa Beatrice Spada Potenziani. It is her descendant, the Principe Giovanni del Drago, a keen gardener, who has created most of the present garden, planting a great range of native flora and exotics that thrive in the island's gentle microclimate. The island is a combination of old woods, pasture and garden, the most cultivated part of which is the *giardino all'italiana*, set in the monastic remains.

The garden has fine collections of roses, camellias, hydrangeas, oleanders, and bamboos. There are also groups of pine, bay, and chestnut, as well as olive, citrus, cherry, fig, and grape. The island's indigenous tree cover of oak, alder, holm oak, limes, and juniper is relieved by maple and mulberry, and exotics include oriental planes, eucalyptus, magnolia, cedars, and palms. The sheer cliffs are home to many native and migratory birds.

Further information from:
Ferry companies. From Lago di Bolsena: Navigazione Alto Lazio Tel: 0761 798033; from Capodimonte: Navigazione "La Bussola" Tel: 0761 870760 or 871115

Nearby sights of interest:
Medieval town of Viterbo, including Piazza San Lorenzo, old quarter of San Pellegrino, Palazzo Papale, and the Museo Civico; Villa Lante; Bomarzo.

The garden on the island of Bisentina is remarkable for its range of native and exotic flora, planted by the present owner, Prince Giovanni del Drago.

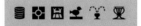

open: All year, daily except public holidays, guided tours every half hour, from 9am to one hour before sunset.

open: Permission must be sought from Soprintendenza of Lazio (06 6798867)

Further information from:
Via J. Barozzi 71, 01031 Bagnaia (Viterbo)
Tel: 0761 288088

Nearby sights of interest:
Bomarzo: Sacro Bosco;
Villa Farnese, Villa Ruspoli at Vignanello; Viterbo.

Bagnaio: Villa Lante

Location: Bagnaio, 5km (3 miles) E of Viterbo

On one of the most important and magnificent gardens in Italy, the Villa Lante dates to the 1560s, when Cardinal Gianfrancesco Gambara started its construction with the architect Giacomo Barozzi da Vignola and the engineer Tommaso Ghinucci. This is a perfect Renaissance garden in which murmuring water, flashing fountains, and shade and sunlight alternating under vast plane trees, together with superb stone carving and the geometrical water parterre at its lowest point, become unforgettable memories.

In the 16th century the town of Bagnaia was the property of the Bishopric of Viterbo and it was the site of the summer retreats of the bishops. In 1568 the Cardinal Gambara laid out his new property, with twin *palazzine* (although the second, western, one was only completed after his death) as simple adjuncts to the

Looking over the parterre to the town from one of the pavilions.

The Montalto arms are held aloft by four naked men in the centre of the water parterre.

The water cascade is a long runnel, shaped as an elongated crayfish, symbol of Cardinal Gambara.

The Fountain of the River Gods, with shell-shaped basins and cornucopias, receives water from the Catena d'Aqua.

garden design, next to the large *barco* (walled hunting park) created by Cardinal Raffaele Riario in 1514. The creation of the garden, the layout of which falls into two parts – the wooded park and the formal garden in which water becomes the main focus – involved great expenditure.

Different from most Italian villas, where the palace is usually at the centre of the composition, at Bagnaia the space is mainly devoted to a sequence of fountains on different levels, while the twin *palazzine* are relegated to a secondary position. The fountains were completed by Carlo Maderno in 1612.

The garden, organized on four levels along a main axis emphasized by the fountains, has perfect symmetry. The lower terrace is divided in 18 square compartments. The four central ones are occupied by pools. Four bridges lead to the island at the centre where the Fountain of the Moors (Fontana dei Mori), comprised of four naked men, hold up the arms of Cardinal Peretti Montalto. In each pool a small ship recalls the *naumachia*, performances representing marine battles, recorded in the literature of ancient Rome. The 12 square compartments around the perimeter, now planted with French-style box broderies, were originally framed by lattice fences and laurustinus *(Viburnum tinus)*, with fruit trees planted along the edges. Herbs and flowers were probably cultivated inside each square.

An overview looking across the water panels and box parterres.

Two flights of steps on both sides of a rectangular slope, over which four diagonal ramps define an almond-shaped rhomboid, lead to the second terrace. This is closed in by a retaining wall with the concave Fontana delle Lucerne at the centre, so named for the 160 jets spouting water from small cups. The terrace is planted with tall plane trees *(Platanus orientalis)*. Twentieth century planting of hydrangeas and camellias around the fountain spoil appreciation of its remarkable architectural form.

On the third terrace the axis is enhanced by the Fountain of the Table. A water runnel in it recalls Pliny the Younger's first century description of dishes floating on water, but was also to cool wine and fruit. Two flights of steps provide access to the third terrace dominated by the monumental Fountain of the River Gods. Here water falls from the upper level into a shell-shaped basin and from this into another one carved with bas-reliefs representing sirens. A large basin collects the water spouting from small cups along the rim into a runnel, carved with a sequence of swans. On either side two colossal reclining River Gods hold cornucopias – symbols of abundance. At their backs stairs ornamented with giant urns reach a slope where, along the central axis, the water flows from the upper level over the Catena d'Acqua, a long runnel shaped as an elongated crayfish – the symbol of Cardinal Gambara. The Chain is fed by the Fountain of the Dolphins, a complex basin, decorated with eagles, harpies, vases and monstrous heads, placed at the centre of the fourth and last terrace. Beyond this plane trees shade the Grotto of the Deluge. A reservoir built with tufa and covered with maidenhair fern is the primary source of the water supply. The water spouts from grotesque heads emerging from three caves into a large basin where two dolphins swim. On both side of the grotto two pavilions, the Loggias of the Muses, have elegant Palladian arches. The inscription on the friezes and the crayfish on the façade recall the cardinal who created the villa.

The hunting park to the side of the garden complex still preserves some original fountains. The most remarkable is the Fountain of Pegasus, its winged horse carved by Giambologna, to the right of the entrance to the garden. A fresco in the west *palazzina* (*c.*1578) shows the Villa Lante and Caprarola and an engraving of 1569 gives evidence that the garden has been preserved almost unchanged since its conception. The Villa Lante remains a landmark in the history of Italian gardens.

Four flights of steps frame the almond-shaped rhomboid, or *mandorla*, that leads to the second terrace.

open: All year, 8.30am to sunset

Further information from:
01020 Bomarzo (VT)
Tel and fax: 0761 924029

Nearby sights of interest:
Medieval town of Viterbo; Villa Lante; Villa Farnese; Villa Ruspoli; Isola Bisentina.

The carved stone "monsters" at Sacro Bosco are placed in the wood. The iconography is obscure but the bearded man represents either Neptune or Father Tiber.

Bomarzo: Sacro Bosco

Location: 15km (9¼ miles) E of Viterbo; A 1, exit Attigliano

The stone monsters of Bomarzo's Sacro Bosco – or "*Parco dei monstri*" has been described as as a uniquely grotesque assemblage of mythical, literary and heraldic sources that have, for generations, baffled and enthralled visitors to Vicino Orsini's remarkable 16th-century park. The *bosco* forms the park to the Castello Orsini, and was begun in the 15th century under the direction of Gian Corrado Orsini. It was, however, not until the tenure of his son Vicino after 1542 that the park acquired its array of giant beasts. The park's rough terrain is strewn with large sculptures set in open glades, or – rather annoyingly – behind modern ranchstyle fencing. The park itself is sparsely treed, although two flanks open into lush, mossy woods that in the early 1900s used to smother the whole site.

The iconography and symbolism of the stone *grotteschi* remain somewhat obscure. We are overwhelmed by the bewildering cast which greet us at every turn – the Elephant with its towering howdah, the Dragon fending off a pride of lions, the giant gaping fish mouth, the colossal mask carved out of the hillside with a table and bench in its jaws, the turtle surmounted by Fortuna, and the Pegasus fountain set upon an expanse of greensward. The great influx of tourists does not, as yet, diminish the unexpected delight of this most eccentric of all Italian gardens.

Caprarola: Villa Farnese

Location: 19km (12 miles) SE of Viterbo

The palace of Caprarola stands at the top of the town, dominating all views and looking out towards Rome. The fortress, originally designed by Antonio da Sangallo, was transformed in the 1570s into a magnificent palace at the behest of Cardinal Alessandro Farnese II, nephew of Pope Paolo III. The building was designed by Giacomo Barozzi da Vignola, who probably also conceived the layout of the garden. The work was continued by Giacomo del Duca and completed by Girolamo Rainaldi in 1620.

The pentagonal building is connected with both the western winter garden and northern summer garden by bridges. Both gardens are square and are divided into four compartments with each compartment further subdivided into another four minor inner squares. In the early 17th century fruit trees and flowers were planted in the beds, but today overgrown box hedges distort the original aspect and hedges of holly and cherry laurel with a smattering of camellias give a different ambiance. From the two terraced gardens a path, passing though a woody area planted with huge shady ilex, chestnuts, pines, and beech, leads to da Vignola's masterpiece, the 1560 *casino*, the Casino del Piacere (House of Pleasure), which appears suddenly beyond a complex sequence of fountains and steps. Two stepped ramps on both sides of a long runnel (Catena d'Acqua) ascend the slope. The water tumbles downstream in a series of small basins carved in the shape of dolphins. The ramps lead to the middle terrace, with the beautiful Fontana dei Fiumi (Fountain of the Rivers). Two flights of steps, curving on both sides of the Fontana dei Fiumi, reach the two gardens framed with 28 male and female statues supporting vases, designed by Rainaldi in 1620. Two other steps, edged by a sequence of dolphins and horses spouting water into small vases, lead to the entrance of the *casino*. Beyond this a large square, paved with pebble mosaic, precedes the original flower garden terraces – still awaiting restoration with authentic plants. The lower terraces are decorated with fountains and stone spheres. The perfect balance between landscape, architecture and sculptural decoration, and the sequence of spectacular features, make Caprarola one of the greatest masterpieces of Italian garden art.

open: All year except 1 Jan, 1 May and 25 Dec, 9am to one hour before sunset; west and north garden can be visited with custodian. The garden of the Casino can be visited only with permission of the Soprintendenza of Lazio (06 369831/6798867)

open: As above

Further information from:
Villa Farnese, Piazza Farnese, 01032 Caprarola (Viterbo)

Nearby sights of interest:
Medieval town of Viterbo; Bomarzo; Villa Lante; Villa Ruspoli; Isola Bisentina; Lago di Vico.

At Caprarola steps from the two square gardens, edged with herms (male and female statues supporting vases), lead up to Vignola's masterpiece, the 1560 *casino*.

open: All year except 1 Jan,
1 May and 25 Dec, 9am to one
hour before sunset
open: As above

Further information from:
Piazza Trento 1, 00019 Tivoli
(Rome)
Tel: 0774 312070

Nearby sights of interest:
Tivoli, including Villa Adriana,
Villa Gregoriana; the city of Rome.

Villa d'Este, Tivoli

Location: 35km (21¾ miles) from Rome, Tiburtina SS 5: A 24 exit Tivoli

Villa d'Este, renowned for its spectacular use of water, represents
the quintessence of the Italian garden of the High Renaissance.
The villa sits above the precipitous garden, but in the garden
every inch of space is controlled by manmade terraces,
flattening out towards the bottom to three tranquil fishponds
and, today, where orchards and covered *berceaux* once made
formal patterns, soaring cypresses form a central rondel.

Created for Cardinal Ippolito d'Este after 1559 by Pirro
Ligorio, the original scheme, although now romantically softened
by evergreen trees and shrubs, still remains. A main central axis
runs down the slope, pierced by a series of cross axes, all linked
by stairways and gently sloping ramps, to reveal views of
sparkling fountains and statues, grottoes and niches. Michel de
Montaigne visited in 1581 before the gardens were finished and
noted how the spray of the fountains made rainbows. In planning
the garden Ligorio derived inspiration from classical ruins but
also incorporated an allegorical theme comparing the d'Este's
harnessing of the water to Hercules' mighty labours and the
cleansing of the Augean stable. Further symbolism includes
fountains linking Venus with profane love and Diana with chastity.

The ingenuity of the water features, including the famous
Organ Fountain – completed in 1661 – and the Walk of the
Hundred Fountains, were based on the hydraulic theories of

The cascade of the Organ
Fountain (begun in 1568) at the
Villa d'Este, with the modern
fountain of Neptune below.

Hero of Alexander in Circa 100 AD. Originally visitors approached from the plain below, but today they go through the lower rooms of the villa – noting early frescoes of the garden by Gerolamo Muziano – on to the highest terrace and a dramatic entrance into the world of sparkling spray and the bewildering sounds of rushing water. The garden is impeccably maintained and the whole water system has recently been restored.

---

8 *Castel Gandolfo*

Location: 25km (15½ miles) S of Rome on Via Appia SS 7

open: By appointment only
open: As above

Further information from:
Direttore de Dene, Ville Pontificio, 00040 Castel Gandolfo, Rome

Nearby sights of interest:
Castel Gandolfo, including Villa Papale (not open to public) and Lago di Albano in the crater of an extinct volcano.

Perched on the the rim of the volcanic crater that is now Lake Albano, the papal city of Castel Gandolfo has a spectacular position and is rich in history. The garden is an extraordinary combination of ordered Italian gardening with walls, ancient and new, avenues of cypress and oak, monumental fountains, and classical statues of great beauty.

In AD 81 the Emperor Domitian shifted his court from Rome and built an elaborate villa overlooking the plain of Latium. Pope Urban VIII built a new residence in 1623, incorporating more land and the imperial ruins into the estate. The property was ceded to the Vatican in 1929 and Pope Pius XI ordered the architect Bonomelli to create an homogenous whole that would respect the layout of the Domitian villa. The prospect from the belvedere on the upper terrace gives views over formal parterres and immaculate lawns, framed by towering cypresses. A statue of Domitian where four cypresses meet is a marvellous *coup de théâtre*. Part of the garden area is a farm that produces food for the religious communities within the papal estate.

The formal parterre at Castel Gandolfo, richly planted with annuals, is framed by impressively tall cypresses.

Giardini della Landriana

Location: Via Campo di Carne 51, Tor San Lorenzo, 50km (31 miles) from Rome

open: Apr to Oct, weekends
9am–6pm; guided tours

Further information from:
For bookings contact:
Administrazione Taverna, Via di
Monte Giordano 36, 00186 Rome
Emanuela Giannuzzi-Savelli; tel 06
91010350, Fax: 06 6876333
DRI-Roma Ente Interregionale,
Via E. Filiberto 17, 00185 Rome;
Tel 06 70497920, 10am–1pm,
3pm–6pm on weekdays

Nearby sights of interest:
City of Rome; seaside resort
of Ostia.

**Russell Page designed some of
the garden compartments at La
Landriana. The white garden
slopes towards the lake.**

This is an amazing 10ha (25 acre) garden, created since 1956, in a
mixture of luxuriant English and controlled Italian styles. For
Italy the planting is eclectic with a multiplication of separate
compartments, thirty two in all, including topiary, flower borders,
colour schemes, a hellebore walk, a formal garden of clipped bay,
an olive garden, a lake, collections of old roses, a cool shaded
hosta garden, and many other themes. The garden is laid out on
different levels and, in spite of the hot summers, with an eye to
providing colour and interest from April to October.

The Marchesa Lavinia Taverna and her husband bought the
derelict farmland in an area near the sea – the old Pontine
Marshes – not far from where Pliny the Younger had his own
Latium villa. For the first ten years the Marchesa experimented
with acclimatizing plants before inviting Russell Page to help her
give the garden "bones". His ideas and layout are still evident,
especially in the Orange Garden, in which today, together with
the Marchesa's plant choices, citrus, clipped with spherical

heads, dominate balls of *Myrsine
africanus* in an unusual formal
pattern. In the olive garden
established trees make patterns of
light and shade over flowerbeds,
planted in a natural cottage style
with flowers of mauve and pale
yellow. The Viale Bianca (White
Garden) follows as a descent down
steps made from local tufa rock,
into the valley, with tulips and
narcissus followed by white and
shell-pink roses, *Gaura lindheimeri*
and other white flowers, as well as
Salvia leucanthae providing a touch
of blue in the winter months.
The Marchesa has spent forty
years extending the garden and
formal and informal "rooms" open
and close in succession to reveal
collections of viburnums and of
magnolias, as well as a field of
Rosa chinensis 'Mutabilis' (now *R.* x
odorata 'Mutabilis'), zantedeschias
and irises growing by the lake,
beyond which she now intends to
plant trees and shrubs chosen
mainly for their autumn foliage.

San Liberato Chiesa Romanica e Giardini Botanici

Location: Bracciano, 39km (23 miles) from Rome, SS 2 N to La Sorta, then SS 493

The church and garden of San Liberato, owned by noted art historian Conte Sanminiatelli, is set on a ledge with magnificent views over Lake Bracciano and the Rocca Romana beyond. Originally the site of a Roman market town among a forest of chestnut trees, a new house was built on the hillside. Russell Page came to work here in 1964 after the garden had been started by Contessa Sanminiatelli. At first Page concentrated on planting around the site of an ancient church, terracing with low walls and narrow paths to make a series of small rectangular beds in medieval style. Planting of grey-leaved shrubs, rosemary and sage, and roses spill out over the path under the olive trees. Formal rose beds edged with *Teucrium fruticans*, clipped as a hedge, counterbalance the churchyard planting and beds of flowering shrubs add interest. Page made the circular courtyard more formal with tightly cut bay hedges and lemon trees in pots.

The arboretum, laid out by Conte Sanminiatelli and Russell Page in an adjacent meadow, is full of interest: tulip trees. pines, black walnut, scarlet oak, magnolias, and maples. Russell Page wrote: "I know of no other garden more magical than this...the simple planes of the gardens, the sloping woods and fields where even the details...have come together in silent harmony."

open: Apr to Nov except Aug by appointment only; guided tours available for groups
open: As above

Further information from:
Via Settevene Palo 33, Loc. S. Liberato, 00062 Bracciano (Rome)
For bookings contact::
Arch. Max Bernard, Tel: 06 99805460 and Fax: 06 9988384

Nearby sights of interest:
Town of Bracciano, including the castle and the lake.

The garden around the old church at San Liberato was laid out by Russell Page with terraces and small rectangular beds.

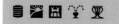

open: Apr to Nov, first Sat and Sun of month; Apr to June, third Sun of month; 1 May; guided visits only

Further information from:
04010 Doganella di Ninfa (LT)
For bookings contact:
Fondazione Roffredo Caetani, Via delle Botteghe Oscure 32, 00186 Rome, 06 68803231 Mon to Fri mornings
Or World Wildlife Lazio, Via Trinita dei Pellegrini 1, 00186 Rome, Tel: 06 6896522, Mon to Fri 9am–7pm, Sat 9am–1pm
Or Lega Italiana Protezione Uccelli, corso Matteotti 169, 04100 Latino, Tel: 0773 488993. E.P.T. Latina, Via Duca del Mare 19, 04100 Latina Tel: 0773 498711

Nearby sights of interest:
Medieval town of Sermoneta; Tempio d'Ercole at Cori.

Giardino e Rovine di Ninfa

Location: 22km (13½ miles) NNE of Latina, 70km (43 miles) from Rome

For many travellers the gardens among the flower-covered ruins of Ninfa, in their romantic profusion of scented roses and jasmines and rushing sparkling water, must represent the ideal of a terrestrial paradise, combining the natural and architectural beauty of the site with an astonishing collection of plants, collected from all over the world, and happily acclimatized in this 9ha (20 acre) garden. Temperatures rarely fall below 10°C (50°F), and generous summer heat and abundant water from the hills make gardening infinitely rewarding. Ninfa is unique and remains many people's ideal of the perfect garden, in which

Giant timber bamboos tower above acanthus in the woods.

The tower of the old fortress is backed by the mountains above Ninfa and looks over the *hortus conclusus*.

The Ponte de Legno over the river is closest to the Municipio building.

The Ponte Romano crosses the river on the main axis of the original village.

nightingales sing and a cacophony of frogs croak in the ponds. The prosperous town of Ninfa already existed in Pliny the Younger's time in the first century AD, and he records a visit there to the temple of the nymphs built over the natural springs. The medieval town, with a cathedral, seven churches, and walls and towers, was sacked in 1382, when the owner Onorato Caetani opposed the pope. The town remained crumbling and abandoned until the 20th century when the Caetanis reclaimed the land, canalized the river, its crystal clear water a home to trout, stabilized the ruins, converted the medieval town hall into a dwelling and made a garden. In 1920 Gelasio Caetani instigated plans to drain the unhealthy marshes.

With his English mother Duke Gelasio began to plant native trees – evergreen oaks, plane trees, pines, cedars, and cypresses, the latter as an avenue down the main street. Soon exotics from America and Asia were added, tulip trees, swamp cypresses and ginkgos, and English-type cottage flowers such as peonies, hollyhocks, lavenders, and buddlejas. His brother Roffredo inherited the property and with his American wife, Marguerite Chapin, further expanded and enriched the garden. Their daughter, Lelia Howard, was an artist and gardener who continued to search out new specimens until her death in 1977.

Even when it lay deserted Ninfa was famous for the wild flowers which spread throughout the ruins and meadows. In the 18th century the German historian Gregorovius described how

Arum lillies have colonized the banks of the river and streams at Ninfa.

"over Ninfa waves a balmy sea of flowers". A hundred years later, in 1874, Augustus Hare saw flowers which "grow so abundantly in the deserted streets, where honeysuckle and jessamine fling their garlands through the windows of every house, and where the altars of the churches are thrones for flame-coloured valerian". Today there are meadows of flowers, a "wild" rock garden in which native and foreign flowers compete – aromatic cistus and sages, erigerons from Mexico, Californian poppies, and early-flowering anemones, crocus and narcissi. Grassy paths are lined with hedges of rosemary and lavender. In the shade carpets of wild cyclamen spread to flower in spring and autumn. Each medieval stretch of wall provides a sheltered microclimate for rare tender plants – caesalpinias with golden flowers, scented trachelospermums, climbing hydrangeas and schizophragmas, the roses 'La Follette' and *R.* x *odorata* 'Pseudindica', alternating with straggling ivy and clematis. Other roses clamber up the trees in the cypress avenue which leads from the cathedral to the river down the main street. Trees planted by Gelasio and his mother have grown vast to give welcome shade, there is a grove of pomegranates, a cluster of Judas trees, a collection of American and Asiatic magnolias, tulip trees in flower in May, the rare *Cladrastis sinensis*, giant bamboos, Chinese bead trees, acers, and tree peonies. Hoherias from New Zealand flourish beside *Drimys winteri* from Chile. Tender pines, *Pinus patula* and *P. montezumae* from Mexico, have soft grey leaves.

Cypresses, often defining the street lines of the medieval village, also provide frames for climbing roses and clematis.

There is also a walled garden under the tower at Ninfa – although this may not be accessible to the general public. Here old formal pools and a flowerbed layout may well reflect some 17th-century gardening activity when an ancestor of the family, Francesco Caetani, was a celebrated plant collector at a time when new bulbous plants from the eastern Mediterranean and plants from the New World were flooding in to western Europe. Today grapefruit, lemons, and beds edged with boxwood reveal a more formal approach than in the rest of the Ninfa gardens. Above all other memories of Ninfa comes the sound of rushing water. Streams are lined with Japanese iris and arums *(Zantedeschia aethiopica)*, while the river is bordered more majestically with giant-leaved gunnera and trailing roses.

Flag iris and gunnera – the giant-leaved *Gunnera manicata* from Brazil – enjoy the moist areas.

Fortunately, the future of the garden seems assured. In recent years the Caetani Foundation have managed to prevent industrial development that would have taken Ninfa's water supply and forever spoiled this special place. The area surrounding the garden was made into a nature reserve by Lelia Howard and her husband, Hubert.

Rome: Villa Borghese

Location: N of city centre, immediately above Piazza del Popolo

open: All year, dawn to dusk, except for the secret gardens
open: As above

Further information from:
00186 Rome
Tel: 06 6832938

Nearby sights of interest:
City of Rome, including Villa Giulia, Galleria Nazionale d'Arte Moderna, Piazza del Popolo and S. Maria del Popolo, Piazza di Spagna, Via del Corso, and the Ara Pacis Augustae (the Augustian altar).

Although the famous gardens of the Villa Borghese have few historical features remaining, it is in the process of restoration.

Although the gardens and park of the Villa Borghese are only a remnant of their past glory they are certainly worth strolling through. Their interest mainly lies in their history. The villa was started in 1608 by Cardinal Scipione Borghese. It included a magnificent palace, 30 fountains, aviaries, hunting pavilions, hundreds of sculptures, gates, and various exedra.

The Casino Nobile, the core of the estate, had on either side two secret gardens, cultivated with rare flowers and espaliered oranges. The surrounding grounds were divided into three walled enclosures. The first one, close to the *casino*, was laid out in 23 compartments planted with holm oaks, pines and spruce along rectilinear avenues decorated with a display of antique statues, hermae, fountains, columns, and seats. The second enclosure, used for deer hunting, had two loggias for receiving the guests and a green exedra decorated with giant hermae. The third enclosure was a large park with hills, woods and glades, and two spectacular clipped *ragnaia* for hunting birds. From the turn of the 18th century to the first decades of the 19th century Prince Marcantonio Borghese and, later, his sons Camillo and Francesco, enlarged the estate and made changes in the park such as the Giardino del Lago (Garden of the Lake), an attempt at an English-style landscape garden. In the middle of the lake is the Temple of Aesculapius, designed by Asprucci. Winding paths were substituted for the 17th-century geometric patterns. By this time the villa was often open to the Roman citizens for feasts and religious ceremonies. In the early 1800s numerous statues were sold to Napoleon by Prince Camillo and many pavilions and buildings were destroyed. Notwithstanding these transformations, Villa Borghese still preserves parts of the general layout, such as the secret gardens beside the *casino* with the aviary designed by Girolamo Rainaldi and the Meridiana pavilion.

In 1901 the villa and the collections were sold to the Italian State and became a public park. The Commune of Rome has started a great restoration programme for the park and the gardens, now in a forlorn condition, to return them to their former glory.

13 *Rome: Villa Celimontana Mattei*

Location: Piazza della Navicella; other entrances from Piazza SS. Giovanni e Paolo

open: All year except 1 Jan, Easter, 1 May, 15 Aug and 25 Dec (*Casino* is address of the Geographical Society for the Study of Mediterranean Archaeolgy)

Once surrounded by magnificent gardens, the original *casino*, designed for Ciriaco Mattei by Girolamo del Duca, was built on the Caelian Hill south of the Colosseum overlooking the Baths of Caracalla between 1581 and 1586. The garden consisted of elaborate box-patterned beds, a series of labyrinths, and *boschetti* peopled with animal statues. In the 17th century the garden was enriched by a series of fountains by Gian Lorenzo Bernini. In the early 19th century the garden became a landscape park, although retaining some fine avenues, and today shade-giving pines, evergeen oaks, palms and lime trees make it a welcome retreat. Fragments of the 16th-century plan survive with an obelisk, a fountain and a theatre.

Further information from:
00184 Rome

Nearby sights of interest:
Rome, including Colosseum, Palatine, Roman Forum, Capitol, SS Giovanni e Paulo, fine view S to the Alban Hills.

14 *Rome: Orto Botanico*

Location: 24 Via Corsini, SW of the centre of the city

open: Daily except Sunday, winter 9am–5pm; summer 9am–7pm

The garden lies beyond the Palazzo Corsini below and on the slopes of the Janiculum Hill. The large building results from the transformations directed by the architect Ferdinando Fuga, appointed by the family Corsini in 1736 after they had purchased the property from the Riario, who had owned it since the 15th century. In 1883 Prince Tommaso Corsini sold the palace to the Italian State and thereafter it became the site of the Academy of Lincei and the Botanical Garden of the University of Rome was established in the grounds.

The lower part of the garden partly preserves the formal layout and some 18th-century features including the *scalone* – flanked by 16th-century plane trees *(Platanus orientalis)* – the Water Chain and Triton's Fountain. There are fine plant collections including dasylirions from Mexico, Arizona and Texas, and a remarkable palm tree area with specimen date palms *(Phoenix dactylifera)*, the canary date palm *(Phoenix canariensis)* and the thread palm *(Washingtonia robusta)* from Mexico. At the foot of the Gianicolo Hill collections of rhododendrons and ferns, a pond with water plants, and more than 60 species of bamboo are arranged in a landscape style with a small Japanese garden. From the top of the hill under the Villa Aurelia a breathtaking view of Rome can be enjoyed. The conservatories are concentrated in the northern end of the garden, one for succulents (Serra Corsini)

Further information from:
Largo Cristina di Svezia 24, 00165 Rome
Tel: 06 6864193
Fax: 06 6832300

Nearby sights of interest:
Rome, including Galleria Corsini, Villa Farensina, and Gianicolo Hill.

In the Orto Botanico of Rome water plants around a pond are arranged in landscape style.

and a collection of orchids in the Monumental Conservatory, built in 1887. In addition to the historic garden, beyond the Via dei Riari there is a recently planted herb garden, and a Tropical Conservatory, built in 1987, devoted to plants that need at least 24° C (75°F) and high humidity. In the central pool a *Victoria amazonica* flourishes. The visitor walking on different levels can admire the plants from various points of view.

open: All year, dawn to dusk; guided visits available
open: As above

Further information from:
00165 Roma. For bookings contact: Museo del Folklore, Piazza S. Egidio, 1/b, Tel: 06 5899359 and 06 5813717

Nearby sights of interest:
Rome, including Villa Farnesina Chigi and the Vatican City.

The formal parterres below the 17th-century casino are fringed with lemon pots.

15 *Rome: Villa Doria Pamphili*

Location: SW of city centre, entrance beyond Porta San Pancrazio

Now a large public park – its perimeter covers 10 km (6 miles) – on the outskirts of the city beyond the Juniculum Hill, the garden surrounds a 17th-century *casino* built for the powerful Donna Olympia Maidalchini by her admirer Camillo Pamphili. Below the *casino* lies a scrolled French-style box parterre fringed with lemons in pots, looking much as it will have done when first laid out over three hundred years ago.

The Janiculum Hill has been recognized as a favoured setting for gardens and orchards since classical times, and the Doria Pamphili garden occupies the site of the garden of Galba, a Roman governor in Andalusia. Alessandro Algardi was involved in the villa construction and in the layout of the *giardino segreto* in 1644, with a Venus *nymphaeum* by Ferrabosco and Snail Fountain by Bernini. After inheriting in 1793 Principe Andrea Doria altered the Baroque style of the outer garden and fountains, softening it into more of a landscape with the addition of a lake and ornamental pools. During the 19th century most of the straight *allées* and avenues were swept away to create an even more pastoral landscape, but many architectural features from the earlier period remain to be discovered. These include an exedra, a Doric temple, and fountains of Regina and of the Tritons – all situated among the umbrella pines, evergreen oaks and exotic palms which give the visitor such admirable shade in the hot Roman summer.

16 *Rome: Villa Farnesina Chigi*

Location: Via del Lungara at the foot of the Janiculum Hill, in Trastevere

The garden around this beautiful villa is modern and of no particular interest but decorations and depictions of flowers by Raphael and *trompe l'oeil* views of the landscape around Rome by Peruzzi, give interest to gardeners interested in history and in the flowers that would have been known at this time.

The simple elegant villa has a Tuscan look, and indeed it was built by Baldassare Peruzzi for the banker Agostino Chigi (who both came from Siena) in the early 16th century. In 1579 it was acquired by Cardinal Alessandro Farnese, who used to entertain in the 17th-century portico that overlooked the Tiber. The loggia and rooms were decorated by such artists as Raphael and his pupils Sebastiano del Piombo, Sodoma and Peruzzi. The frescoes in the loggia show garlands of flowers and fruit, while Psyche's room shows the story of her love affair with Apollo.

The original garden was embellished with classical statues, discovered in recent excavations. Today the garden is more or less a romantic pleasure ground but parts of it, still laid out with box hedges, together with a shady arbour of bay, have formal overtones.

open: All year except Easter Sun, 1 May, 15 Aug and 25 Dec, Mon to Fri 9am–2pm, Sun 9am–1pm

open: As above

Further information from:
Via della Lungara 230, 00165 Rome
Tel: 06 6886565

Nearby sights of interest:
City of Rome, including quarter of Trastevere and churches of Santa Maria, Santa Cecilia, and view over city from Janiculum Hill.

---

17 *Rome: Orti Farnesiani*

Location: Through Forum off Via di San Gregorio, or from the Via del Fori Imperiale

Although few plants – excavations have destroyed their terraced sites – and virtually no buildings, except for de Vignola's aviaries, remain to mark the site of this historic 16th-century botanic garden, it should still be a stop on any garden itinerary in Rome. Built for Pope Paul III by da Vignola between 1534–39, with twin aviaries above triple terraces, it was filled with all the rarieties then obtainable. *Acacia farnesiana*, introduced in 1611 from the island of San Domingo, was grown in the garden. Other plants new to Europe included yuccas and agaves (*Agave americana* flowered for the first time in Rome), passion flowers, the camphor tree from the east, tuberose from Mexico *(Polianthes tuberosa)*, and the Atamasco lily *(Zephyranthes atamasco)*. A catalogue, written by Pietro Castelli, *Exactissima descriptio rariorum quarundum plantarum, quae continentur Romae in Horti Farnesiano* (1625), is an important source for our knowledge of plants known and grown in 17th-century Rome which still has great relevance to today's horticulturists.

open: Jun to Sep, daily except Tue 9am–7pm; Oct to Mar 9am–5pm Sun and public holidays 9am–1pm; closed 1 Jan, 1 May, 25 Dec

Further information from:
Via del Fori Imperiale, 00186 Rome

Nearby sights of interest:
Rome, including the Forum.

Magnificent views over Rome can be seen from the garden.

open: All year, daily
9am–7pm; to 1.30 pm on Sun and
public holidays
open: (Etruscan Museum) All
year, Tues to Sat 9am–7pm; Sun
9am–1pm

Further information from:
P. le di Villa Giulia 9, 00196 Rome
Tel: 06 322 6571
Fax: 06 3202010

Nearby sights of interst:
City of Rome, including Villa
Borghese and Galleria Nazionale
d'Arte Moderna.

Rome: Villa Giulia (Villa di Papa Giulia)

Location: On the fringe of the Villa Borghese park

Although the garden of the villa has almost disappeared, its original design and architecture were of great influence in the development of many late 16th- and 17th-century Italian gardens. The whole ensemble is still beautiful. Set among thick woods, the construction, begun in about 1550, was commissioned by Pope Julius III, and planned by Dal Monte, Ammanati, Vasari, and da Vignola, the most important architects of the time. Their respective contribution to the design is difficult to identify. Da Vignola probably contributed the loggia in the courtyard at the back, from which curving balustraded steps lead down to a sunken *nymphaeum* and fountain. Today the hermae in the small grotto in the *nymphaeum*, and the remarkable pavement made of marble indicate the quality of the original decoration.

The layout of the first courtyard, flanked by wings and decorated with statues in niches, is in the shape of a "U", inspired by Bramante's belvedere courtyard at the Vatican. A stunning portico in Mannerist style leads to the loggia, second courtyard and *nymphaeum*. Originally there was a vegetable garden and a vineyard. Today the only "live" gardening are Renaissance-style box hedges, with bay trees, roses and oleanders. Under the umbrella pines, modern groundcover of Japanese lily turf *(Ophiopogon planescens)* keeps the garden cool and fresh.

At the Villa Giulia the sunken *nymphaeum* is still preserved in its orginal 16th-century form.

19 *Rome: Villa Medici*

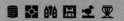

Location: On Pincian Hill at top of Spanish Steps

The basic 16th-century layout at the Villa Medici still survives, although wooded compartments, hedged with ilex, bay and box since the 18th century, give a romantic wooded appearance very different from the low-growing parterres originally laid out. The villa was purchased in 1576 by the Cardinal Ferdinando de' Medici. Ferdinando was interested in creating a garden where he could display his collections of antique sculptures and marbles.

The original garden of simples and flowers – camomile, roses, poppies and peonies – was laid out in front of the inner rear façade. In the northern area cross paths delineated 16 compartments, edged with *Viburnum tinus*, in which dwarf fruit trees were planted. On the south side a stair led to a terrace garden, where a *ragnaia* was once planted. Beyond this an artificial hill represented Mount Parnassus. Famous Roman sculptures, such as the Group of Niobides (now at the Uffizi) ornamented the grounds. Since 1804 the villa has belonged to the French state and houses the French Academy established by Napoleon. Velasquez painted at the villa in 1649–50. In 1873 Henry James described the garden as "perhaps ... the most enchanting place in Rome ... with a long mossy staircase climbing up to the Belvedere, rising suddenly out of the leafy dusk".

open: Guided visits by appointment only

Further information from:
Viale della Trinità dei Monti 1,
00187 Rome
Tel: 06 676 11 and 679 8381

Nearby sights of interest:
City of Rome, including Villa Borghese, the Spanish Steps and Keats-Shelley Memorial House, and the church of Santa Maria del Popolo.

The statue of Parnassus with attendant muses and the winged horse Pegasus in the 16th-century gardens of the Villa Medici.

🍁 20 *Rome: Vatican Gardens*

Location: Behind Basilica di San Pietro, Vatican City

open: By appointment only
open: (Vatican museums) All year, Mon to Sat and Sun of each month 8.45am–1.45pm; Easter period and 1 July to 30 Sept Mon to Fri 8.45am–4.45pm, Sat 8.45am–1.45pm

Further information from:
Vatican State tourist office

Nearby sights of interest:
City of Rome, including the Vatican City, Piazza San Pietro, Basilica di San Pietro, Vatican Museums, and Castel Sant'Angelo.

The Vatican is a whole city of gardens, with schemes that include well maintained parterres, rock gardens and even woodland and, above all, several dramatic views of the dome of St Peter's. There are two areas of particular interest in the history of garden design and architecture. Although buildings now occupy most of the site, Bramante's early 16th-century revolutionary design can still be identified. He organized a magnificent central perspective that traversed the rising terraces at right angles, linking them by a series of ramps and staircases, ending in a semi-circular niche. Two vast loggias enclosed the area, with triple, double and single arches to give architectural form to the terraces. The garden became a setting for fountains and sculptures (now in the Vatican Museum). The other major historical feature in the gardens is the Villa Pia, built in the 1560s by Ligorio – a *casino* surrounded by a shady *bosco* – for Pope Pius IV. Of classical inspiration, the façade is decorated with mosaics in grotesque style and stucco work bas-reliefs depicting mythological scenes, overlooking a courtyard and fishpond.

Much of the rest of the Vatican Gardens have an English landscape look, with winding paths, flowerbeds, a modern parterre, some attractive arches of *Trachelospermum jasminoides*, and commemorative plantings of tree specimens.

The Villa Pia in the Vatican Gardens was designed by Pirro Ligorio in the 1560s and built as a retreat for Pope Pius IV.

Castello Ruspoli

Location: Vignanello, 15km (9 miles) from Viterbo

open: All year, Sun
10am–2pm

Further information from:
01039 Vignanello (VT)

Nearby sights of interest:
Medieval town of Viterbo,
including Museo Civico; Villa
Lante; Villa Farnese; Bomarzo.

Formal parterres, perhaps the oldest surviving in Italy that retain their original early 17th-century geometric layout, are overlooked by the castle to which it is joined by a bridge over a sunken road. The severely classical design of the parterres is attributed to Marcantonio Marescotti, who had married Ottavia, the daughter of Vicino Orsini, creator of the Sacro Bosco at Bomarzo (p.100). Originally planted as flowerbeds the designs, based on the initials of Octavia and her sons, are in box but may originally have had their formal lines delineated in rosemary, santolina and other herbs. The beds would have provided sites for many of the bulbs, corms and rhizomes newly introduced from Constantinople and the Middle East in the 16th century.

Originally a Benedictine monastery and then a fortified castle, Ruspoli was transformed into a domestic villa for the Orsini family in 1574. The parterres, set in a flat rectangular space between wings of evergreen oaks, are set out in twelve patterns of box, each surrounded by clipped bay, with pots for lemons on each corner. Two straight *allées* separate the parterre patterns into groups of four. Well maintained and with the box lines clipped and crisp, this garden, off the main Italian garden itinerary, is well worth a short detour if it can be fitted in to the rather restrictive Sunday opening hours.

The Castello Ruspoli has the oldest extant parterre in Italy, laid out at the end of the 16th century.

Key to gardens

1 Palazzo Reale and the English Garden
2 Orto Botanico, Catania
3 Villa Trinita
4 La Mortella
5 Il Biviere
6 Santa Chiara
7 Orto Botanico della Reggia, Naples
8 Orto Botanico dell'Università, Naples
9 Orto Botanico, Palermo
10 Parco della Favorita
11 Villa Giulia
12 Villa Malfitano
13 Villa Palagonia
14 Imperial Villa Casale
15 Villa Cimbrone
16 Villa Rufolo
17 Casa Cuseni
18 Villa Madonna della Rocca

Key

═══ Motorways
═══ Principal trunk highways
③ Gardens
⬤ Major towns and cities
● Towns

Garden tours

━━━ Naples tour: 1, 6, 7, 8
━━━ Sicily tour: 17, 18, 3, 2, 5

The South: Naples & Sicily

In southern Italy – from Naples south to Sicily – the climate, suitable for olives, oranges and lemons, is also very favourable for tender exotics. The soil in the Campania around Naples is particularly rich and fertile, bearing four crops each year, a fact that was certainly appreciated by the Romans. The ancient geographer Strabo reasoned, as has now been proved by scientific analysis, that it owed its fertility to the volcano Vesuvius. And as Pliny the Elder observed in his *Naturalis Historia*, it is also well drained.

Lady Walton's garden on Ischia (pp.124–127) is well protected and, in the valley with rich alluvial soil from the extinct volcano on Ischia, it is possible, with irrigation, to grow tropical specimens, as well as tree ferns and metrosideros from New Zealand, while on the cliffs above native flora flourish. At Pompeii, drowned in lava in 79 AD, many gardens have been excavated. Some, with the help of contemporary wall paintings, have been reconstructed, although little is certain about the plants grown there. In the main it is assumed that with adequate water

The marble fountain by Canart in the Orto Botanico della Reggia in Portici, Naples.

supplies (brought by aqueduct) most plants mentioned in the Roman treatises on agriculture and the writings of both Pliny the Elder and Pliny the Younger will have grown. These included ivy, clipped box, laurel, myrtle, acanthus and rosemary, with citrus fruit in pots.

The most important architectural garden is Vanvitelli's 18th-century Palazzo Reale at Caserta (p.122), modelled on Versailles. Here, a visit can encompass the vast garden and take in the "experimental" late 18th-century English garden alongside, established for the Austrian born Queen Maria Carolina, sister of the ill-fated Queen Marie Antoinette of France, who wanted a garden to rival her sister's Petit Trianon. Strolled in by Nelson and Emma Hamilton and painted by Jacob Philip Hackert with a backdrop of Vesuvius, the English Garden with its exotic trees, yuccas and magnolias is definitely worth visiting.

In Sicily, although we know from descriptions that the Saracen emirs and Norman kings (who conquered Sicily in 1091) laid out luxuriant hunting parks around Palermo "like a necklace which ornaments the throat of a young girl", nothing now remains of even the vast space surrounding the Norman Palace of La Zisa. The pleasure gardens vanished and even the extravagant 18th-century country villas at Bagheria have succumbed to neglect. Among modern gardens only the Casa Cuseni (p.138) has any pretension to a classical design.

Today the gardens of Sicily are mainly of interest for the richness and variety of their plants. It rains during the growing season in winter but all growth effectively stops during the hot summers with mean temperatures of over 25ºC (79ºF). The mild climate makes it possible to acclimatize many tender species – giant Moreton Bay figs and banyan trees, palms, cycads, and cactus.

One of the 19th-century pavilions that enrich the famous Giardino Giulia in Palermo.

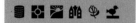

open: All year, daily except
1 Jan, 1 May and 25 Dec
9am–dusk

open: All year, Mon to Sat
9am–1.30pm Sun 9am –12.30pm

Further information from:
Viale Dohuet 2/A, 81100 Caserta

Nearby sights of interest:
Medieval village of Caserta
Vecchia; Roman remains at
Santa Maria Cápua Vetere.

Caserta: Palazzo Reale and the English Garden

Location: Turn E at the Juno Fountain in the Vanvitelli Park behind the palace

Green lawns, hornbeam hedges, and a string of fountains, arranged in Baroque French-style for the Bourbon Spanish Charles VII to rival the gardens of Versailles, stretch for 3km (2 miles) behind the great palace, ending up at the 78m (200ft) cascade and basin of Diana and Acteon, where tumbling water falls over massive blocks of stone, the water brought 50km (31 miles) by aqueduct from Mt Taburno. Although the space is vast and the project partly unrealized, nevertheless it is still possible to grasp the majesty of the idea and to conjure up an image of allegorical statues, triumphal arches, water cascades and *broderie* of flowers and pebbles, designed by Luigi Vanvitelli, that were intended to complete and humanize the layout. Vanvitelli was reponsible for the design of the great rectangular palace between 1752–74, continuing but never completing the garden after King Charles's abdication in favour of his eight-year-old son, who became Ferdinand IV. The garden, begun in 1762, was continued by Vanvitelli's son, Carlo, until 1779.

The English Garden at Caserta was laid out for Ferdinand IV's wife, Queen Maria Carolina, during the last part of the 1780s. Adjacent to Vanvitelli's Baroque garden, it was intended to be a complete contrast, with naturalism as its principle theme. The garden was not only to be a pleasure ground but exotic trees, fruits, and agricultural crops were to be grown as part of a scheme for experimental acclimatization.

With the help of Sir William Hamilton, the British envoy in Naples, the 23ha (57 acre) garden was laid out within an encircling wall by John Andrew Graefer. By 1793 he had established native and exotic trees amid green glades, with a lake and, with entry through a dark cave, the "*bagno di Venere*", with a marble statue of Venus. One of the first camellias in Europe was planted in the garden. Graefer also had an interest in native plants and there were flower gardens, a nursery area, a stove house and greenhouses for tropical and semi-tropical rarities. Today, magnificent magnolias, tulip and camphor trees, palms and eucalyptus, ginkgos and taxodiums, nolinas and yuccas, all take advantage of the site.

The Fountain of Eolo. Vanvitelli installed five successive waterfalls on the wide lawns, flanked with hornbeams that stretch for 3km (1 mile) north of the palace.

Catania: Orto Botanico

Location: Enter from either Via Longo, off Viale Regina Margherita

open: All year, daily
8am–1pm

Further information from:
Direttore Prof. Francesco Furnari
Via A. Longo 19
Tel: 095 430901
Fax: 095 430902

Nearby sights of interest:
Catania, including Villa Trinita,
Giardino Bellini, Piazza del
Duomo, and Castello Ursino.

Although the University of Catania is one of the oldest in Europe, founded in 1434, the botanic garden was only created in 1858 by the botanist Francesco Tornabene. Nevertheless trees have grown with such speed that the originally open space in the centre of Catania is now a shady *bosco*. For the visitor the garden is divided into two parts, the Orto Generale containing mostly exotics that grow in the lava soil from Mt Etna, and the Orto Siculo with indigenous species. Visually most memorable are a pair of large dragon trees *(Dracaena draco)* and Agavaceae underplanted with aspidistra, flanking the garden side of the Institute. Huge agaves, towering clumps of aloes and cycads are well represented, although shade cast by large evergreens, including *Ficus* species, *Araucaria bidwillii, Cocculus laurifolius,* and *Magnolia grandiflora*, make new plantings of sun-loving plants difficult. There are over forty different types of palms, including the date palm *Phoenix dactylifera, P. canariensis, Washingtonia filifera* and *W. robusta*, species of *Sabal*, and native *Chamaerops humilis*. The native plants includes a vast specimen carob *(Ceratonia siliqua)*, a holm oak *(Quercus ilex), Vitex agnus-castus*, and a jujub tree *(Zizyphus jujuba)*.

Dragon trees outside the
Institute in the Orto Botanico.

Catania: Villa Trinita

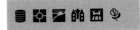

Location: Via Trinita, above the city of Catania

open: By appointment only

Further information from:
Azienda Agritoristica Trinita,
Via Trinita 34, 95030 Mascalucia
Catania
Tel and fax: 095 7272156
Mobile: 0337 955493

Nearby sights of interest:
Historic Catania, including Orto
Botanico, Giardino Bellini, Piazza
del Duomo, and Castello Ursino.

Laid out on the slopes of Mount Etna, the garden, surrounded by mandarin groves, has many mature plants. Salvatore Bonajuto not only maintains the original planting but continues to expand, especially with native plants, including typical Mediterranean *macchia* plants. Here native trees such as *Quercus pubescens*, aromatic pistacias and feathery fennel remind one of the vanishing countryside. Near the house old boxwood hedges provide a sense of privacy, with jasmine, begonia, passion flowers, and plumbago. The Australian silky oak, *Grevillea robusta*, Chinese bead tree *(Melia azedarach)*, and *Jacaranda mimosifolia* and *Phytolacca dioica* from South America indicate botanical enthusiasm. *Solanum rantonettii* and *Polygola myrtifolia* thrive here with no protection, while a collection of bulbs: alliums, narcissi, and *Scilla peruviana*, grow in an open area. In another "room" there is a selection of palms. Old shrub roses and irises extend the flowering seasons. Sig. Bonajuto is planting deciduous oaks, and aloes and agaves survive in a sheltered pocket.

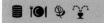

open: Easter (or earlier) to
Oct, Tue, Thu and Sat, 9am–7pm

Further information from:
Fondazione William Walton, Via
E.Calise 35, 80075 Forio, Isola
d'Ischia (Na)
Tel and Fax: 081 986237

Nearby sights of interest:
Ischia Porto and Ischia Ponte.

4 *Ischia: La Mortella*

Location: Boat to Porto Ischia from Naples or Pozuoli

A massive gate off a dusty lane leads to an oasis of
greenery, where spray and bubbling water keeps
the air humid enough to grow magnificent tree
ferns (*Dicksonia antarctica* and *Cyathea dealbata*
from New Zealand). The European chain
fern *(Woodwardia radicans)* also thrives.
There is a host of rare and tender trees,
palms, shrubs, ferns, and bulbs, a
dazzling array of good things to excite
the plantsman and botanist. La Mortella
is not only a garden of lush exotics but
part of its charm lies in the parallel
existence of indigenous plants, clinging to
the steep terraced hillsides above and
scenting the air with the familiar
aromatic fragrance of the *machi*a.
Umbrella pines, groves of ilex and
arbutus, Italian cypress, bay, *Quercus
coccifera*, myrtles (from which the name
Mortella comes), Spanish broom,
buckthorn, *Erica arborea*, cistus, pistacia
(*Pistacia lentiscus* and *P. terebinthus*),

An Islamic-type rill of water leading
to a pool was part of Russell Page's
extension of the garden.

Lady Walton's skilful planting
complements Russell Page's design
to make an unforgettable impression.

The main pool, flanked with giant volcanic rocks, is almost a natural feature.

The fountain that completes the axis of the L-shaped garden looking towards the main rock pool and jet.

dome-shaped *Euphorbia dendroides* in flower in March, phlomis, rosemary, cyclamen carpeting the ground in shade and caper plants in sun cascading out of the crevices of rocky walls.

The composer William Walton and his wife Susana came here in 1956, starting the garden in the sloping gully before they begun building the house in 1962 – set back into the hillside, facing the setting sun above the valley garden. The designer Russell Page drew up a plan for the south-sloping valley, allowing the rocky ground to dictate the seemingly naturalistic planting style but imposing his own geometry, an axial line running south with the valley from the largest egg-shaped pool, framing the distant peak of Mt Ipomeo. This main vista links pools and planting themes, and combines with a second axis, almost at right angles, allowing a western view focused on a fountain. A group of staccato cypresses make a vertical accent. Forty years on, his design, elaborated over the years with an Islamic rill and an octagonal pool, emphasizes the garden as a work of art, a combination of rigid geometry with exuberant and luxuriant planting. To show the depth of the gentle sloping gully, trees were planted as bones around its perimeter and to flank the entrance drive. Umbrella pines *(Pinus pinea)*, Judas tree *(Cercis siliquastrum)*, the ancient fossil tree *(Ginkgo biloba)*, camphor *(Cinnamomum camphora)*, as well as jacarandas and a bombac *(Chorisia speciosa)* from Lady Walton's Argentinian homeland, and soaring incense cedars *(Calocedrus decurrens)* from North America, many grown from seed by Susana Walton who, inspired by Russell Page, quickly became a talented and very knowledgeable plantswoman with a sure eye for planting detail.

A grove of tulip trees *(Liriodendron tulipifera)*, today grown tall, were planned to provide central shade, essential for establishing plants in the hot climate, and two other exotics, evergreen New Zealand Christmas trees, *Metrosideros excelsus*, flank a view of the western fountain. Reservoirs were constructed to collect rainwater and the large volcanic boulders were broken up and rearranged as a combined rock and water garden, the largest and most dramatic to remain bare of planting, natural sculpture setting the character of the garden. Russell Page advised establishing small trees better to withstand gales and massing exotic shrubs, ferns and bulbs in large naturalistic groups.

The garden planting reflects Susana Walton's skill and knowledge. Besides the elegant tree ferns, the plant collection in the damp valley demonstrates her vision. Apart from establishing camellias

In the valley plants have grown to make dense vegetation and create microclimates that allow tropical plants to flourish.

in any existing shade, for the first few years only silver-leaved sun-lovers or native plants could survive the summer heat. But as the trees grew denser it was possible to introduce shade-loving plants, and bog plants and aquatics. Now alocasias, gingers, arisaemas, brugmansias – which may flower through the seasons – arums, bletilla, hostas, and zantedeschias, provide exotic flowers and foliage, with drifts of self-seeding *Geranium palmatum* from Madeira, with crimson-centred pink flowers, shade-tolerant hellebores, and acanthus. In full sun, just below the house, a collection of cycads and palms, including the blue-fan palm *Brahea armata* from California, as well as agaves and aloes, furcraeas, the rare *Puya berteroniana, Beschorneria yuccoides, Nolina recurvata* and the dragon tree *(Dracaena draco)* create a sculptural plant garden. A lone *Arbutus* x *andrachnoides* with peeling red-brown bark stands sentinel by the house, between twining jasmines, acacias, and trachelospermums.

The natural rock "rearranged" around the pool below the house provides the dominant structure to the fountain and pool.

On the west-facing cliffs above the gully, steep steps and horizontal paths on stone wall terraces lead to a hidden swimming pool, and a centre for visiting professors and students, and then to the dominating rock which holds Sir William's ashes. In the alkaline soil and heat indigenous plants predominate, enriched by agapanthus, crinums, ixias and belladonnas *(Amaryllis belladonna)* from South Africa, echium from the Canaries, *Pardancanda norrisii* that seeds everywhere, underplanted with species alliums, muscari, and daffodils. A pool above, the Crocodile Cascade, recirculates water. Higher still in the wood and stretching to the edge of the property, Lady Walton has constructed a series of rock pools, their banks a home for bog plants, ferns, and bamboos, a lush green vegetation, in contrast to the parched Mediterranean hillside. A new project is to construct a greenhouse to house the giant waterlily *Victoria amazonica*.

One of the pools in the main axis. The constant humidity created by the fountains makes it possible to grow tree ferns from New Zealand.

The garden, often a setting for William Walton's music, is charged with an extraordinary atmospheric beauty, perhaps part of Sir William's legacy to his wife, who made the garden for his pleasure and repose, while continuing its dynamic growth into the 1990s and beyond.

open: By appointment only

Further information from:
Azienda Agricola, 96016 Lentini
Tel and Fax: 095 783 1449

Nearby sights of interest:
The ancient city of Lentini.

Lentini: Il Biviere

Location: From Catania take SS 385 to Palagonia and Scordia. After 7.3km
(4½ miles) take left turn to Valsavola

Near the ancient Greek site of Leontini, the modern Lentini, Heracles is said to have laid out a lake, teeming with fish and wildlife. For centuries a malarial swamp, thirty years ago it was drained and in 1970 remarkable garden was created. In the raised flowerbeds a collection of succulents flourish, sheltered from winds by Aleppo pines *(Pinus halepensis)* – agaves, aloes, cactus, yuccas, cycads, dasylirions, and euphorbias *(Euphorbia canariensis)*. Although a garden of great botanical interest, the layout has a formal air, with a series of "rooms", linked with sloping banks that change the levels. There are giant cactus, soaring furcreas, *Yucca rupicola* and *Y. elephantipes*, and the rare *Xanthorrhoea arborea* from Australia.

The soil is enriched by volcanic lava from Mount Etna; it is in this region of Sicily that the best blood oranges are grown. Besides the succulents, more conventional plants add seasonal flowers and scent. Feathery jacarandas, a specimen *Parkinsonia aculeata*, the pepper tree *(Schinus molle)*, *Grevillea robusta*, and the bombax *(Chorisia speciosa)*. Roses include *Rosa* x *fortuniana*. *Acca sellowiana* (syn. *Feijoa sellowiana*) produces fruit, and jasmines and plumbago twine over walls. A large Morton Bay fig, *Ficus macrophylla*, has grown quickly in the fertile soil. Poplars, *Populus tremula*, assembled in groves, draw the eye and provide shade, as does a "wood" of *Phoenix canariensis* by the pool. This is a garden of delight, planted with discretion and botanical erudition.

At Il Biviere the Princess Borghese has assembled an amazing collection of "dry" plants.

Naples: Cloisters of Santa Chiara

Location: Strada Santa Chiara, Quartiere di Spacca-Napoli, Naples

open: All year, daily
8am–12pm
open: As above

Further information from:
The Church of the Poor Clares,
Strada Santa Chiara, Naples

Nearby sights of interest:
Naples, including Museo
Archeologico and the old quarter
of Spacca-Napoli.

Behind the 14th-century Gothic basilica of Santa Chiara church in the centre of Naples, the cloisters of the Poor Clares surround an extraordinary garden in which pillars embellished with Capodimonte *faience* tiles depicting flowers and fruit make cross pergolas, interrupted by high-backed benches "painted" with landscape scenes. The pergolas were created by the architect Domenico Antonio Vaccaro in 1742. The church was damaged during World War II but recently restored. The garden pergolas are in the process of a grand programme of restoration.

The columns supporting the wisteria- and vine-clad pergolas are octagonal in shape, covered with glazed tiles by Giuseppe and Donato Massa, decorated with swags of fruit in mainly blue, yellow and green tones. The benches depict Neapolitan life at sea and in a monastery, with landscape scenes of countryside and enclosed gardens in which raised flowerbeds surround a fountain. In two "centres" tall cypresses are a feature – in one shading stone benches, in the other flanking a fountain. The garden planting is attractively domestic with broad beans, broccoli, shallots, and rocket, presumably grown for the monks at the adjacent monastery of the Minor Friars. Olive and orange trees, eucalyptus, irises, borage, bay trees, *Zantedeschia aethiopica*, and roses, give the garden scent and colour, the flowers perhaps used for altar decoration, as was the case in medieval monasteries.

In the Cloisters of Santa Chiara
the columns of the 18th-century
vine and wisteria-covered
pergolas are faced with glazed
tiles portraying swags of flowers
and fruit.

129

open: By appointment only, Mon to Fri, 9am–1pm

Further information from:
Via Universita 100, 80055
Portici (NA)
For bookings contact: Istituto di
Botanica Tel: 081 274356

Nearby sights of interest:
Naples, including Orto Botanico
dell' Universita.

Naples: Orto Botanico della Reggia

Location: 12km (7½ miles) from Naples, A 2 NA-SA exit at Casello di Ercolano

Originally part of the park of the great Baroque palace constructed by King Charles III in 1736, the walled garden was developed as the botanic garden of the Faculty of Agriculture at the University of Naples "Frederico II" after 1872. It consists of two walled enclosures and greenhouses for collections of tender tropical and desert plants, hidden behind the palace (now the Institute of Botany), although its actual perimeter incorporates the remains of a complex pattern of avenues of evergreen oak *(Quercus ilex)* that criss-crossed the original park, the Parco Gussone. The dark oaks enclose the sunlit walled gardens on three sides giving the approach an air of mystery.

The main walled garden is divided into four quadrants, at the centre a marble fountain by Canart surrounded by a pavement design in terracotta, marble and *piperno*. There are many rare and interesting plants in the borders and flowerbeds. Tea olive *(Osmanthus fragrans)* from the Far East and the even more richly scented *Acokanthera oblongifolia* from Africa grow against the south-facing wall. Specimen *Yucca elephantipes*, the yucca-like *Dasylirion quadrangula* with its square stems, a grove of aloes, the jelly palm, *Butia capitata* (syn. *Cocos capitata*) from South America, and a dragon tree *(Dracaena draco)*. A plan exists to restore the garden.

In the greenhouses in the second enclosure there are collections of succulents originating from both the Old and New Worlds, from the families of Cactaceae, Euphorbiaceae, Apocynacee, Asclepiadaceae, Didieraceae, Liliaceae and Crassulaceae. One greenhouse contains a collection of plants from Madagascar. In the shade of the oak tree avenues many indigenous plants of the region have made a natural home: phillyreas, pistacia, smilax, arbutus, *Erica arborea*, bay, honeysuckle, laurustinus, *Acanthus mollis*, butcher's broom *(Ruscus aculeatus)*, and *Ruscus hypoglossum*.

The Orto Botanico della Reggia, surrounded by avenues of evergreen oak from the original palace layout, is in two walled areas with formal axes and views.

Naples: Orto Botanico dell'Università

Location: Via Foria in the centre of Naples

On arrival at the main gate and staircase to the garden, the first view is disappointing, with an avenue of ragged palms *(Washingtonia filifera)* and plane trees. Huge Morton bay figs *(Ficus macrophylla)*, specimen *Quercus ilex*, and a fine *Quercus acutissima*, and dahoon holly *(Ilex cassine)* grow in the grass. But perseverance brings reward. In the eastern corner of the garden there is an astonishing collection of tree ferns, with naturalistic water features, and a humid atmosphere introduced by high sprays. A central area has palms and cycads, another section is of succulents and euphorbias from desert regions, another concentrates on citrus, while a Mediterranean section, although overgrown, has a fine selection of plants. The mild climate makes it possible to grow plants from many parts of the world, including subtropical regions. In the greenhouses there is an important collection of the more tender cycads. The Museum of Palaeobotany and Ethnobotany is also worth a visit.

The gardens were first inaugurated by a decree of Joseph Bonaparte (Napoleon's brother) in 1807 and today are owned by the Faculty of Science at the University of Naples "Frederico II". About 10,000 different species grow in the gardens and the scientific research programme is the foremost in Naples.

open: By appointment only Jan to Jun, Sep to Dec, Mon to Fri, 9am–2pm; guided tours available

Further information from:
Via Foria 223, 80139 Napoli
Tel: 081 449759 and 455654

Nearby sights of interest:
City of Naples, including Santa Chiara and Orto Botanico della Reggia.

The Orto Botanico dell'Univiersità in Naples has excellent collections of palms, cycads cactus, and other "dry" plants, as well as a damp fern garden.

Palermo: Orto Botanico

Location: Via Lincoln in the SE of Palermo

open: All year: Mon to Fri 9am-1pm, Tue and Thu 9am–5pm (6pm in summer)

Further information from:
Via Lincoln, 90123 Palermo
Tel: 091 6161493
Fax: 0916176089

Nearby sights of interest:
Palermo, including Villa Giulia, Palazzo di Normanni, Piazza Pretoria, and Piazza Bellini.

The Orto Botanico in Palermo has an interesting collection of exotics.

Founded between 1779–95, the Orto Botanico has developed a remarkable collection of plants from the tropics and subtropics, including giant fig trees from Asia and Australia, a "forest" of aloes (mainly *Aloe arborescens*), a section containing indigenous Mediterranean plants, and an area for useful plants, the latter including cotton (*Gossypium* species), *Bohemeria nivea* – grown for textiles, soya *(Soya hispida)*, and *Sorghum saccaratum*.

The earliest part of the garden, nearest to the neoclassical buildings of the Gymnasium and Herbarium, is a quadrant bisected by cross *allées* of palms (including *Washingtonia robusta, Phoenix dactylifera* and *P. canariensis*, sabal, and chamaerops), and specimen *Cycas revoluta*. A circular pond, built in the 1790s by Filippo Palatori, is divided into concentric sections of different depth for aquatic plants, which include lotus *(Nelumbium nucifera)*, waterlilies and papyrus. Palms and tropical trees make a dramatic impact, alternating with filtered sunlight, allowing Mediterranean acanthus, the invasive *Oxalis pres-caprea*, and paper-white daffodils *(Narcissus papyraceus)* to give seasonal interest. A vast fig, *Ficus magnolioides (F. macrophylla)*, dominates one end of the garden, with the Indian banyan *(Ficus benghalensis)* and *Ficus rubiginosa* nearby. An avenue of bombac, the false kapok *(Chorisia insignis)* has an underplanting of crinums and variegated tradescantias. Other notable trees include the dragon tree *(Dracaena draco)*, the soap tree *(Sapindus mukorossi)* and a cork oak *(Quercus suber)*. The Mediterranean flora area is especially attractive in spring with both woody and soft-stemmed euphorbias (*Euphorbia dendroides* and *E. ceratocarpa*), *Phlomis* species and bulbs such as *Urginea maritima*. Under Professor Raimondo the garden is being restored, and scientific research by his team emphasizes the uses of plants for medicine and agriculture.

Palermo: Parco della Favorita e Giardini della Palazzina Cinese

Location: Piazza Niscemi, 3km (1 mile) from the centre of Palermo

Laid out as a hunting park and for agricultural experiments by Ferdinand IV in 1799, and named after the royal palace at Portici near Naples, La Favorita has some interesting features. Many of the original statues and fountains have disappeared but, with woods of mainly Mediterranean evergreens, the gardens are a green oasis in the middle of the city, providing a cool retreat during the summer months. The Scuderie Regie (Royal Stables) have been restored and are now an ecological station. At the main entrance, off the Via Duca degli Abruzzi, Ferdinand and his queen, Maria Carolina (sister of Marie Antoinette), built the Chinese-style yellow and terracotta Palazzina Cinese, designed by Venanzio Marvuglia. Nelson and the Hamiltons attended parties here with the royal family. Today the much neglected *palazzina* is closed to the public.

open: All year, daily except Thu, 8am or 9am–2pm; public holidays 9am–1pm

open: Under restoration

Further information from:
Palermo tourist office

Nearby sights of interest:
Palermo, including Orto Botanico.

The Palazzina Cinese was built in the 18th century by Ferdinand IV.

Palermo: Villa Giulia

Location: Via Lincoln in the SE of Palermo

The Villa Giulia was originally laid out in 1778 by Niccolo Palma in a formal pattern, with eight main avenues lined with trees, bisecting the main square, and a central fountain. Goethe visited the garden in 1787, describing it "as the most wonderful spot on earth ... it seems enchanted and transports one back into the ancient world". Besides espaliers of lemons and high hedges of oleanders covered with red blossoms, Goethe found "strange trees" that "spread out their peculiar ramifications". Another visit further stimulated Goethe's ruminations in his search for the "Primal Plant" (see p.52).

The gardens are decorated by 19th-century pavilions and fountains in a slightly unkempt way. According to Murray's *Handbook* of 1864 the garden was "the favourite lounge of idle Palermians", although its most memorable vistor was Goethe, who came to read and write among the newly planted trees. Lemon blossom still scents the air in spring and Goethe's palms and exotic trees are now enormous. Although the geometrical plan is maintained, Judas trees, jacarandas, plane trees, and *Ficus benjamina*, appear in more random style between the flowerbeds.

open: All year, daily 9am–8pm

Further information from:
Via Lincoln
90123 Palermo

Nearby sights of interest:
Palermo, including Orto Botanico, Giardino Garibaldi, church of La Magione, and Galleria Regionale.

open: All year, daily except Sun and public holidays, 9am–1pm; guided tours available

open: As above

Further information from:
Fondazion Giuseppe Whitaker
167 Via Dante, 90141 Palermo
Tel: 091 682 0522
Fax: 091 681 4156

Nearby sights of interest:
Palermo, including church of Sant'Agostino.

At Villa Malfitano, originally owned by the Whitaker family, the collection of exotics is outstanding.

12 *Palermo: Villa Malfitano*

Location: Via Dante NW of the centre of Palermo

The gardens of Malfitano are maintained by the Whitaker Foundation. The Whitaker family has been responsible for some of the most important collections of plants in Palermo and the park of Malfitano, laid out in a landscape style with formal elements after 1885, remains the most important. Nowadays the walled garden consists of four instead of the original seven hectares (10 from 17 acres), but the rich subtropical flora, combined with an attractive layout, remains unique in Sicily.

The garden, basically a landscape park with individual botanical specimens displayed in a gardenesque style, has a formal section behind the house, overlooked by rampant wisteria, and *Rosa banksia* and *R.* 'Marechal Niel' draped over the portico. Two marble lions by Rutelli flank the steps. The formal beds, shaped in a double helix, with paths radiating from a central fountain, were originally underplanted with eupatoriums, but given architectural interest with palm trees (the date palm *Phoenix dactylifera*, *P. canariensis* and *P. reclinata*, and *Washingtonia filifera*, as well as the indigenous *Chamaerops humilis*) and cycads *(Cycas revoluta)*.

Near the front of the house a vast *Ficus magnoloides* (the Australian banyan *F. macrophylla*) was planted in the 1890s. Eclectic planting demonstrates the mild climate where frosts are unknown, although northern winds can bring snow in winter. Today cedars, pines, cypresses, and palms shade flowerbeds that contained perennials in the time of the garden's heyday. Flowering laurustinus, *Pittosporum tobira*, and hedges of *Duranta erecta* look less exotic than the towering pines, yuccas and cycads. Other trees and palms were brought from Australia *(Araucaria bidwillii)*, New Caledonia *(Aurucaria rulei)*, while groves of aloes flowering in winter, *Yucca elephantipes* and rare nolinas *(Nolinia recurvata, N. longifolia* and *N. stricta)* from Mexico, and a dragon tree *(Draceana draco)* all thrive in the mild climate, surviving their comparative neglect. Today the tufa-stone grotto lined with shells is beginning to deteriorate, and the kitchen garden is abandoned to weeds. Nevertheless, a trio of gallant gardeners struggle where a team of 14 once worked. The garden in its luxuriant maturity provides a rare experience for the English visitor. Fortunately, the last of the Whitakers, Delia, created a non profit-making foundation to ensure the future of both the villa and the garden.

13 Palermo: Villa Palagonia

Location: 16km (10 miles) E of Palermo by A 19

The grandest villas of the 18th-century nobility of Palermo were built on their estates in Bagheria, a nearby seaside village. Villa Palagonia, the "villa of the monsters", is one of the few open to the public. The Baroque villa, built in 1715 for Prince Francesco Ferdinando Palagonia Gravina, is famous for its grotesque statues of local tufa stone. These, representing mythological figures, warriors, musicians and dwarfs, besides various deformed figures, hunchbacks and dragons, are arranged along the encircling wall and flanking the two gateways. The villa is now unromantically approached through a dusty garden of palm trees and pines, oleanders, cycads and araucarias, remnants, it seems, of grander gardening days. In fact even when Goethe visited in 1787 he described the "paving ... overgrown with grass and the courtyard ... like a dilapidated graveyard". Although vandalized and weathered, the "monsters" are remarkable. Goethe considered the villa "bad taste and folly of an eccentric mind". The main concave façade has a dramatic double staircase leading to the *piano nobile* and an entrance hall frescoed with the Labours of Hercules. The ballroom is magnificent with a ceiling of "angled" mirrors which distort the viewers below. Walls covered with glass to resemble marble, *trompe l'oeil*, and portraits of the Palagonia family, together with the "monsters", make the visit unforgettable.

open: All year, daily
9am–12.30pm, 4pm–7pm
open: As above

Further information from:
Piazza Garibaldi, Bagheria
Tel: 091 93 20 88

Nearby sights of interest:
Bagheria; Graeco-Roman town of Solunto; town of Termini Imerese.

A double staircase was the original entrance to the Villa Palagonia.

14 Piazza Armerina: Imperial Villa Casale

Location: Casale, 5km (3 miles) SW of Piazza Amerina, central Sicily

The magnificent mosaics found in this luxurious Roman AD 4th-century villa are justifiably famous and worth a special visit. Less well known is the excavated peristyle garden located in the centre of the villa complex. Originally surrounded by marble columns with Corinthian capitals, the rectangular garden has semi-circular pools at either end of a larger almost rectangular tank with a central fountain. Roman peristyle gardens were planned to form an inner room in a house, separated from the outside world, and beyond the open atrium. In the open space, enclosed by shady walks, shrubs and flowers were planted around a central water feature. In the Imperial Villa native plants that may well have been part of the original garden include symmetrically placed clipped bay trees, lentiscus and box.

open: All year, daily,
9.30am–6pm
open: As above

Further information from:
Piazza Armerina tourist office
Tel: 0039 935 68 0201 or 1310

Nearby sights of interest:
Town of Piazza Armerina; town of Caltagirone (noted for its ceramics).

135

open: All year (with cloisters and crypt) 9am to dusk

open: Cloisters and crypt open as above

Further information from:
Via Santa Chiara 26, 84010
Ravello (SA)
Tel: 089 857459

Nearby sights of interest:
Ravello, including Villa Rufolo, the cathedral, the church of San Giovanni del Toro, and panoramic view on road from Amalfi.

The terrace overlooking the Amalfi coastline at Villa Cimbrone is flanked with a series of busts of Roman emperors.

Ravello: Villa Cimbrone

Location: Walk from Piazza Duomo to Via Santa Chiara in central Ravello

The site of the Villa Cimbrone on a clifftop promontory with magnificent views to the Amalfi coast and land falling sharply to the Mediterranean below, is beyond compare. At the entrance steep steps lead up to a an imposing wooden gateway that reveals a long view to the horizon and distant Temple of Ceres, the dramatic central axis of the garden. A wisteria-clad pergola stretches almost the whole length, with side gardens, formal and informal, a rose garden and a bedding-out garden lying to each side. Umbrella pines overhang the pathway, while plane trees, cypresses and olives intermix with cycads, palms, phormiums,and yuccas. Today's air of slight neglect and casualness has a pleasing effect, with grassy swards of native euphorbias, Algerian irises, bulbous asphodels and sea squills *(Urginea maritima)*, scented violets and anemones, and giant fennel *(Ferula communis)*, while *Cyclamen hederifolium* and acanthus carpet the ground under ilex and arbutus, striking a relaxed note.

The, probably 12th-century, villa had fallen into disrepair when it was purchased in 1904 by Lord Grimthorpe. It was restored by Nicola Mansi with a mixture of styles, including typical Edwardian features – temples, a grotto and dark pond, winding paths darkened by laurustinus and *Cocculus laurifolius*,

native and exotic specimens planted within an Italian-style layout. In 1917 Mansi restored a 14th-century cloister, built a neo-Byzantine tearoom, and placed sculptures throughout the garden. A pergola west of the main axis is clothed with Banksian roses and underplanted with hydrangeas. The goddess Ceres shelters under a *glorietta* at the end of the main vista, and the belvedere beyond is flanked by 18th-century busts of emperors.

16 *Ravello: Villa Rúfolo*

Location: Walk from Piazza Duomo to Piazza Vescovado in centre of Ravello

This is a garden within a complex of remarkable early buildings, in which on the lowest of three terraces, jutting out over the steep valley, colourful bedding-out schemes of annuals in formal style vie with specimens of palms, cycads and yuccas. On the top terrace exotic evergreens and box (both *Buxus sempervirens* and *B. balearica*), hedges of euonymus, tall *Cocculus laurifolius*, scented *Pittosporum tobira*, aucuba, myrtle and fuchsias, grow in the shade under tall umbrella pines with adjacent dripping grottoes and fountains, while bright bouganvillea clothe the sunny walls. On the middle level an oleander walk frames the view over the coast.

One of the oldest surviving palaces in Italy, the Villa Rúfolo dates from the 13th century when it was built for the Rúfolo family, and incorporating Saracen and Norman styles in its scattered towers and buildings. In 1851 it was bought by a Scotsman, Frances Neville Reid, a diplomat in Naples and collector of Roman antiquities, and was restored by Michele Ruggiero with great respect for the original fabric. Today the villa is occupied by the European University Cultural Centre. The poet and writer Boccaccio came here during his exile from Florence in the 14th century and described the setting in one of his stories in the *Decameron*. Wagner also visited the villa in 1880 and was inspired to write the dream of Klingsor's magic garden for his opera *Parsifal*. A tree-lined entrance (*Tilia platyphyllos*) leads from a medieval gate tower to the Moorish cloisters from which the tour of the garden can begin.

open: All year, Oct to May 9.30am–1pm, 3pm–5pm; Jun to Sep 9.30am–1am, 3pm–7pm
open: As above

Further information from:
Piazza Vescovado, 84010 Ravello
Tel: 089 857657 and 857669

Nearby sights of interest:
The town of Ravello, including Villa Cimbrone and the cathedral.

At Villa Rúfolo the wide terrace is planted as a formal garden with palms, yuccas and cycads.

17 *Taormina: Casa Cuseni*

Location: Via Circonvallazione in the town of Taormina

⇼ open: By appointment only

Further information from:
7 Via Circonvallazione, Taormina
Tel: 094 22842

Nearby sights of interest:
Resort of Taormina, including Villa
Madonna della Rocca Teatro
Greco, Giardino Pubblico, view
over Gulf of Taormina from Piazza
9 Aprile, and the Castello.

At Casa Cuseni the planting
complements a beautiful design
and the garden, in this favoured
climate, is always full of flowers.

The lovely house and gardens of Casa Cuseni were built by
Robert Kitson in 1907. On a steep slope, with a spectacular view
of Mount Etna and the sea, the garden has a distinctive English
atmosphere. Here a series of formal geometric rooms, some
distinguished by pebble mosaic patterns (*ciottolato*) and decorated
with old Tunisian tiles, are linked by steps and ramps, and
planted with a profusion of tender plants tumbling over pathways
and walls. Kitson probably designed the house himself, and
planned the garden aligned on geometric terraces set parallel to
the house walls to take advantage of the views and microclimate.
His niece, Daphne Phelps, has loved and tended the garden
since his death in the early 1950s.

Arriving involves a steep ascent from the entrance gates
through an orchard of citrus; lemons, grapefruit, mandarins,
and sweet oranges. Architectural features, devised by Kitson,
are incidents along the way. A small basin and dripping water
is backed with Rococo decoration, walls are stencilled with
caricatures of the owner and his builder, and a double staircase
leads to the house terrace. Two small formal gardens are reached
from the side door of the house. In one santolina and lavender
edge flowerbeds planted mainly with
bulbous spring-flowerers, while in the
second irises predominate. Behind the
house a secret garden, paved with
ciccolato, is planted sparingly. The final
triumph is a swimming pool on the
highest terrace, festooned with wisteria,
and reflecting Mount Etna in its surface.

Plants reflect a taste for collecting,
stretched over nearly a hundred years.
The almond trees blossom in early
spring, sheltering the exotic glaucous-
leaved *Beschorneria yuccoides*. White
wisteria and bouganvillea curtain the
pergola. *Echium candicans* and *Geranium
maderense* grow next to scented paper-
whites *(Narcissus papyraceus)*, red flax,
freesias, and *Jasminum polyanthum*, with
snowdrops and cyclamen flourishing in
shady corners. In places native
Mediterranean plants have found their
own niches. Asphodels are already in
bloom in January, *Centaurea taorminia*,
bay, myrtle, acanthus, euphorbias, pink-
flowered *Convolvulus althaeoides* and the

blue *C. sabatius* trail and clamber over walls and neighbouring plants. Some rare trees and shrubs add extra spice to more pedestrian plantings of eriobotryas and Judas trees. *Lagunaria patersonii* from Australia, scented *Acokanthera oblongifolia* from Africa and *Erythrina crista-galli* from South America all enjoy the climate. There is much beauty – the site alone must be one of the most magnificent in Europe.

⁙ *Taormina: Giardino Villa Madonna della Rocca*

Location: Via Circonvallazione in the town of Taormina

Laid out at the turn of the century by an Austrian and now owned by his granddaughter, the hanging gardens are steeply terraced, allowing views to the Greek theatre to the east of Taormina and the sea on the west. Walls have been constructed in grey stone from local quarries, mixed occasionally with stones of black lava. The original owner was a collector of antique marbles, arches and other artifacts which, now romantically entwined with creepers, decorate the garden. Planting is rich and diverse. Pepper trees *(Schinus molle)*, jacarandas and Italian cypresses now shade plantings of *Dasylirion longissima*, cycads and agaves *(Agave attenuata)*. The paths are fringed with Algerian iris *(Iris unguicularis)*, with both white and lavender flowers, crinums and periwinkle. Native myrtles, giant fennels and acanthus contrast with the exotics. A Chinese parasol tree, *Firmiana simplex* (syn. *Sterculia platanifolia)*, first grown in the English Garden in Caserta in the 18th century, thrives in the rich tufa soil.

open: By appointment only

Further information from:
Via Circonvallazione 41, Taormina
(Messina)
Tel: 094 415 777
Mobile: 0337 955493
(Marina Simili)

Nearby sights of interest:
Taormina, including Casa Cuseni, Teatro Greco, Giardino Pubblico, view from Piazza 9 Aprile over Gulf of Taormina, and the Castello.

The garden of Madonna della Rocca is rich with exotics while natives, such as acanthus, fennel and myrtle, thrive in the shade.

Glossary

allée Walkway bordered on either side with plants, usually trees or hedges.

ampiteatro Flat or gently sloping area surrounded by abrupt slopes.

barco A walled hunting park.

Baroque Style of artistic expression, prevalent in 17th century, marked by elaborate ornamentation and forms.

belvedere Ornamental building that commands an extensive view.

berceau Tunnel, arch or arbour that supports climbing or trained plants.

bosco, boschetto Wooded area in a garden.

broderie Ornate parterre with designs that imitate embroidery patterns.

casino Ornamental house within a garden.

claire-voyée View through a hedge or wall at the end of an *allée*.

cottage orné Small rustic building used as a feature in an ornamental garden.

exedra Open garden building, usually semicircular in shape and with seating.

fattoria A farmhouse or farm building.

giardino inglese "Garden in the English style". A garden with informal arrangement of shrubs, lawns and trees popular in England in the 18th century.

giardino all'italiana "Garden in the Italian style". Usually refers to a formal layout of parterres arranged around a fountain.

giardino segreto Walled garden associated with the Italian Renaissance.

giochi d'acqua Games or jokes such as water jets designed to entertain garden visitors.

glorietta Ornamental pavilion, usually in the middle of a walled garden.

herm Head or bust on a stone pillar or pedestal.

isolotto Small decorative island within a garden.

limonaia Glasshouse that protects potted citrus trees in cold weather.

loggia Roofed open gallery behind a colonnade or arcade.

macchia Mediterranean bush or scrub.

Mannerism Artistic movement in Italy, *c.*1520–1600. It aimed for greater impact and brilliance than Renaissance style.

nymphaeum Grotto with fountains dedicated to nymphs.

*palazzina (*pl. *palazzine)* Small villa.

parterre Regular ornamental beds with low-cut hedges of either flowers or turf, often incorporating decorative devices such as urns or topiary.

patte d'oie Arrangement of three *allées* or avenues radiating from a central point.

piano nobile Main floor of a house, usually the first floor.

piazzale Square or similar open space.

plate-band A border to a parterre in the form of a narrow flowering bed.

*putto (*pl. *putti)* Cupids or cherubs.

ragnaia Wood where nets for trapping birds were once stretched over trees.

rocaille Decoration of shells or rocks often found on the walls of grottoes.

rond-point A circular clearing in woods or parks where a number of *allées* meet.

salone Hall or assembly room.

scala Stairs or staircase.

trompe l'oeil Painting or ornament that appears to be something it is not.

viale An avenue.

Biographies

Alberti, Leon Battista (1404–72) Florentine architect whose reinterpretation of classical Roman ideals influenced Renaissance architecture in Europe.

Algardi, Alessandro (1602–54) Italian architect, sculptor and decorator who worked in Venice, Rome and Naples.

Bernini, Pietro (1562–1629) Influential Florentine sculptor who worked in Rome and Naples.

Bramante, Donato (1444–1514) Italian architect of the Renaisssance who worked chiefly in Rome.

Buontalenti, Bernardo (1536–1608) Florentine architect and engineer, celebrated for the "spectacles" he designed for the Medici and his decoration of grottoes.

Fontana, Carlo (1638–1714) Italian architect, a pupil of Bernini, who worked mainly in Rome but also designed Isola Bella on Lake Maggiore.

Giambologna (Giovanni da Bologna) (1529–1608) Mannerist architect and sculptor who worked mostly in Florence.

Goethe, Johann Wolfgang von (1749–1832) German poet, novelist and dramatist. Considered the founder of modern German literature.

Japelli, Giuseppe Early 19th-century neo-classical Italian architect and garden designer who worked at the Villa Emo in the Veneto.

Juvarra, Filippo (1685–1735) Sicilian architect, a pupil of Carlo Fontana, who worked in Milan and in Tuscany at the Villa Mansi and the Villa Reale.

Le Nôtre, André (1613–1700) French garden designer who influenced garden design throughout Europe. His work includes Versailles and Vaux-le-Vicomte.

Ligorio, Pirro (c.1510–83) Neapolitan architect and painter who worked in Rome and at the Villa d'Este in Tivoli.

Michelozzi, Michelozzo (1396–1472) Florentine architect and sculptor whose work for the Medici family included the Villa Medici at Fiesole.

Page, Russell (1906–85) English garden designer who worked in Italy, England, France, and Spain and wrote the influential book *The Education of a Gardener* (1962).

Palladio, Andrea (1508–80) Venetian architect and author of *Quattro libri dell'Architettura* (1570).

Peruzzi, Baldassare (1481–1537) Sienese architect and painter who worked mostly in Rome

Pinsent, Cecil (1884–1964) English architect and garden designer who worked in Italy, England and Yugoslavia.

Pliny the Elder (AD 23–79) Roman scholar. His works include include the encyclopedic *Historia naturalis*.

Pliny the Younger (AD 61–112) Roman statesman and adopted son of Pliny the Elder whose letters include descriptions of the gardens at his villas by Lake Como and north of Rome.

Rainaldi, Girolamo (1570–1655) Roman architect who worked at the Villa Borghese and the Palazzo Farnese.

Sangallo, Antonio da (the Younger) (1485–1546) Florentine-born architect who trained under Peruzzi and Bramante and worked in Rome.

Tribolo, Niccolò (1485–1550) Florentine sculptor who worked for Cosimo de' Medici at the Boboli Garden.

Vanvitelli, Luigi (1700–73) Neopolitan architect who worked in Rome, Ancona and Naples. He designed the original garden of the Palazzo Reale at Caserta.

Vignola, Giacomo Barozzi da (1507–73) Italian architect who created many of the finest landscape designs around Rome, including the Villa Giulia, the Villa Lante and the Villa Farnese.

Index

A

Acton, Arthur 77
Acton, Sir Harold 77
Adriana, Villa 94
Agliè, Castello del 16
Agliè, Count Filippo d' 16
Albani, Count 86
Alberti, Leon Battista 60
Albertolli 23
Aldobrandini family 63, 94
Aldobrandini, Villa 36, 94
Algardi, Alessandro 112
Allegri-Arvedi, Villa 44, 46
Ammannati, Bartolommeo 60, 68, 71, 114

B

Bacciochi, Elisa 60, 82, 83
Bagatti Valsecchi, Villa 18
Bagnaio see Villa Lante
Balbianello, Villa del 18
Balze, Le 68
Barbarigo, Antonio 47
Barbarigo Pizzoni Ardemani, Villa 8, 44, 47
Barbaro, Daniele 44, 52
Barbaro, Villa 43–44
Belgioioso, Villa 10
Berenson, Bernard 79
Bernini, Gian Lorenzo 19, 51, 66, 86, 111, 112
Bettoni, Villa 49
Bianchi, G.B 46
Biviere, Il 128
Boboli Garden 60, 68–69
Bomarzo: Sacro Bosco at 94, 100, 117
Bonafede, Francesco 52
Bonajuto, Salvatore 123
Bonaparte, Joseph 131
Bonaparte, Napoleon see Napoleon I
Borgaro, Birago di 16
Borghese family 110
Borghese, Villa 10, 110
Borromeo family 30–33, 34
Bozzolo, Villa della Porta 8, 35
Bramante, Donato 9, 91, 114, 116
Brenzone, Villa 44
Brignoli, Giovanni 40
Brivio-Sforza, Villa 19
Buonaccorsi family 62
Buonaccorsi, Giardino 62
Buontalenti, Bernardo 60, 68, 69, 78
Burnet, Bishop Gilbert 32

C

Caetani, Francesco 92, 108, 109
Calderara, Marquis 22
Canonica, Luigi 39
Canzio, Michele 28
Capponi family 70, 73
Capponi, Villa 70
Capra, Villa 43
Caprarola, Villa Farnese 92, 101
Caprile, Villa 85
Carlotta, Villa 20
Caroline of Brusnswick 22, 85
Casabona 88
Casa Cuseni 120, 138-9
Caselli, Count 72
Caserta, gardens of 10, 120, 122
    Palazzo Reale and the
        English Garden 120, 122
Castel Gondolfo 103
Castelli 32
Castello Gardens 60, 71
Catajo, Castello del 48
Catania, gardens of 123
    Orto Botanico 123
Celimontana Mattei, Villa 111
Celle, Parco 72
Celsa, Castello di 63
Certosa di Pontignano 89
Cetinale, Villa Chigi 9, 10, 64–67
Charles VII, King 122
Chigi family 64, 66, 67, 113
Ciani, Baron Gianpetro 21
Cicogna, Count Gianpetro 21
Cicogna Mozzoni, Villa 14, 20–21
Cimbrone, Villa 136–37
Cipressi, Villa 22, 25
Cocker, Henry 37
Como, Lake, gardens of 14, 18–27
Contini, Giovan Battista 62
Corsini, Corsini 72
Cortenova, Lelio Mornico di 24
Cortile del Belvedere 9, 91
Cusani, Marquis Carlo 40

D

del Drago, Principe 95
del Duca, Girolamo 111
Demidoff family 78
Doria, Prince Andrea 112
Doria Pamphili, Villa 112
Duchêne, Henri 77
Durazzo Pallavicini, Villa 28
Durini, Cardinal 18

E

Emo, Contessa Giuseppina 48
Emo, Marina 48
Emo, Villa 48–49
Este, Cardinal Ippolito d' 102
Este, Villa d' 9, 22, 102–103

F

Fabroni, Cardinal Agostini 72
Farnese family 101, 113
Farnesina Chigi, Villa 113
Favorita, Parco della 133
Fedorovna, Empress 22
Ferdinand, Archduke 39
Florence, gardens of 8, 59, 60, 68–78
Foce, Villa La 80
Fontana, Carlo 32, 64, 66, 67
Frascati 92, 94
Frietsch, Joseph 78

G

Gambara, Cardinal 96
Gamberaia, Villa 73
Garda, Lake, gardens of 43, 49–50
Garzoni, Villa 60, 81
Genga, Girolamo 86
Genoa 8, 28, 29, 38, 40
Giambologna 69, 76, 78, 99
Giulia, Villa (Palermo) 133
Giulia Villa (Rome) 114
Giusti, Giardini 44, 57
Goethe, Johann Wolfgang von 52–53, 57, 133, 135
Gori, Giuliano 72
Graefer, John Andrew 122
Grimaldi, Parco Villa 29
Guicciardini Corsi Salviati, Count Giulio 74
Guicciardini Corsi Salviati, Villa 74

H

Habsburg family 14
Hadrian, Emperor 94
Hamilton, Emma 120
Hamilton, Sir William 122
Hanbury, Sir Thomas 17
Hanbury, Giardini Botanici see La Mortola
Heller, Andre 50
Howard, Lelia 108, 109
Hruska, Dr Arturo 50
Hruska Botanico, Giardino 50

I

Imperial Villa Casale 135
Imperiale, Villa 86
Ischia see La Mortella
Isola Bella 10, 30–33
Isola Bisentina 95
Isola Madre 32, 34

J

James, Henry 115
Japelli, Giuseppe 10
Jelinek, Antonio 55
Julius II, Pope 9, 91
Juvarra, Filippo 41, 81

K

Kitson, Robert 138
Kress, Walter 24

L

Lambton, Lord 9, 64, 67
Landriana, Giardini della 92, 104
Lante, Villa 92, 96–99
Le Nôtre, André 84
Lentini *see* Il Biviere
Ligorio, Pirro 92, 102, 116
Lucca, gardens of 59, 60, 81–84

M

McEarchern, Neil 37
Madonna della Rocca, Villa 139
Maggiore, Lake, gardens of 8, 10,
    13, 30–37
Malfitano, Villa 134
Manin, Ludovico 51
Manin, Villa 44, 51
Mansi, Nicola 136–37
Mansi, Villa 60, 81–82
Marches, The, gardens of 58–90
Marchi, Marcello 73
Maria Carolina, Queen 120, 122,
    133
Maria Theresa, Empress 39
Massei, Villa 83
Mattei, Ciriaco 111
Maximilian, Archduke 44, 55
Medici family 59–60, 68, 71, 75,
    76, 78, 115
Medici Gardens (Florence) 9
Medici, Villa (Fiesole) 75, 87
Medici, Villa (Rome) 115
Melzi, Villa 23
Michelozzi, Michelozzo 60
Miralfiore, Villa 86
Mirafiore, Emanuele di 76
Miramare, Castello di 44, 55
Monastero, Villa 24–25
La Mortella 119, 124–127
La Mortola 13–14, 17
Mozzoni, Angiola 21
Mozzoni, Ascanio 21

N

Naples, gardens of 10, 119, 129
    Orto Botanico della Reggia 130
    Orto Botanico dell'Universita 131
Napoleon I, Emperor 32, 39, 51,
    66, 82, 110, 115
Negrotto Cambiaso
    Pallavicino, Parco Villa 38
Nelson, Horatio 120
Ninfa, Giardini di 92, 106–109

O

Origo, Iris 80
Orsini family 100, 117

P

Padua 10,
    Giardino Botanico 44,
        52–53, 88
Page, Russell 104, 105, 126
Pagni, Raffaello 76
Palagonia Gravina, Prince 135
Palagonia, Villa 135
Palermo 120
    Orto Botanico 132
Palladio, Andrea 43, 48
Pallavicini, Marquis Ignazio
    Alessandro 28
Pallavicino, Marchesa Luisa Sauli
    38
Pallavicino, Marques Tobia 38
Pallavicino, Villa 36
Palma, Niccolo 133
Parigi, Giulio 68
Paul III, Pope 92, 95, 113
Pecci Blunt, Countess 83
Peruzzi, Baldassare 60, 63, 92, 113
Pesaro, gardens of 86
Petraia, Villa della 60, 76
Phelps, Daphne 138
Piazza Armerina *see* Imperial Villa
    Casale
Pienza 87
Piccolomini, Palazzo 87
Pietra, Villa La 77
Pinsent, Cecil 68, 70, 75, 79, 80
Pisa 10, 44, 59, 60, 88
    Orto Botanico 10, 44, 60, 88
Pisani, Villa 10, 44, 53
Pizzo, Villa 25
Pizzoni Ardemani, Count 47
Pliny the Younger 14, 26, 99, 104,
    106–108, 120
Pompeii 119–120
Pratolino, Villa 8, 78

R

Rainaldi, Girolamo 101, 110
Rainieri, Archduke 25
Ravello, gardens of 136–137
Reale, Villa (Marlia) 60, 82–83
Reale, Villa (Monza) 39
Rizzardi, Conte Antonio 54
Rizzardi, Villa 44, 54
Rome, gardens of 60, 90–117
    Orti Farnesiani 113
    Orto Botanico 111–112
Rúfolo family 137
Rúfolo, Villa 137
Ruspoli, Castello 117

S

Sangallo, Antonio da 101
San Liberato Chiesa Romanicae e
    Giardini Botanici 105
Sanminiatelli, Conte 105

San Remigio, Villa 36
Santa Chiara, Cloisters of 129
Santini, Marchese Nicolao 84
Saxe-Meiningen, Duchess of 20
Scamozzi, Vincenzo 48
Scott, Lady Elisabeth 70
Semplice, Giardino dei 78
Serbelloni, Duke Alessandro 26
Serbelloni, Villa 27
Serra di Comago, Parco 40
Sforza, Alessandro 86
Sicily, gardens of 10, 119–120, 123,
    128, 132–135, 138–139
Siena 9, 60, 63, 64, 67, 89
Sorra, Marchioness Ippolita 40
Sorra, Villa 40
Spence, William Blundell 75
Strong, Charles Augustus 68
Stupinigi, Palazzo di 10, 14, 41
Suarez, Diego 77

T

Taormina, gardens of 120, 138–139
Taranto-Ente, Villa 37
Tatti, Villa i 79
Taverna, Marchesa Lavinia 104
Tivoli 9, 92, 94,102–3
Tornabene, Francesco 123
Torrigiani, Villa 60, 84
Trezza, Luigi 54, 57
Tribolo, Niccolò 60, 68, 71,
    76, 78
Trieste 44, 55
Trinita, Villa 123
Trissino Marzotto, Villa 56
Turin 8, 10, 14, 16, 41
Tuscany, gardens of 58–89

V

Vallombrosa, Duke of 36
Vanvitelli, Luigi 120, 122
Vasari, Giorgio 68, 114
Vatican Gardens 116
Venaria Reale, Villa 8
Veneto, gardens of the 47–48,
    52–53, 56
Venzano 89
Verona 44, 57
Vignola, Giacomo Barozzi da 92,
    96, 101, 113, 114
Villoresi, Ettore 25
Vittorio Emanuele II, King 76
Von Ketteler, Mrs 73

W

Walker, Ella 27
Walpole, Lady Elisabeth 75
Walton, Lady Susana 119, 126–27
Walton, Sir William 126, 127
Wharton, Edith 70, 73
Whitaker family 134

Acknowledgements

I am so grateful to Giorgio Galletti for helping me with this book, writing some of the descriptions, and adding so much to it with his historical knowledge. I must also thank Todd Longstaffe Gowan for his inspiring contributions and many others who have helped me on the way. The book has come alive with the pictures, most of which were taken especially by David Markson. I would also like to thank Michèle Byam, senior editor at Mitchell Beazley, and the rest of her team for contributing their skills.

Penelope Hobhouse, *September 1997*

Photographic Acknowledgements

Front and back jacket: Reed Consumer Books Limited/David Markson
Inside back flap: Andrew Lawson Photography

t=top; b=bottom; c=centre

Raffaello Bencini, Florence 72. Garden Matters 83. Garden Picture Library/Lamontagne 25, /John Ferro Sims 73, 80, 103. Studio Giancarlo Gardin, Milan 51, 55. Jerry Harpur 6c, 65t, 67. Penelope Hobhouse 19, 22, 46, 54, 66t. Image Bank/Andrea Pistolesi 69. Todd Longstaffe Gowan 64, 65b. Tony Mott 16, 63, 70, 77, 86, 98, 112. Hugh Palmer 44/5, 62, 71, 96t, 97b, 99, 100, 101, 125t. Marcella Pedone 53. Charles Quest-Ritson 17, 23, 36, 79, 87, 124, 125b, 127t, 133. Reed Consumer Books Limited/David Markson 1, 2/3, 5, 5, 7, 8, 9, 10/11, 13, 14/15, 18, 20, 21, 24, 26, 27, 28, 29, 30, 32, 33, 34, 35, 37, 38, 39, 40, 41, 43, 47, 48, 49, 50, 52, 56, 57, 60/61, 66 (bottom), 68, 74, 75, 76, 81, 82, 84, 89, 92 /93, 94, 95, 102, 104, 106, 107t, 107b, 107c, 108, 109b, 109t, 110, 113, 114, 115, 116, 117, 119, 120/121, 122, 123, 124b, 126, 127b, 128, 130, 131, 132, 134, 135, 136, 137, 138, 139. Agenzia Fotografica Luisa Ricciarini, Milan/Roberto Schezen 97t. Franca Speranza Agenzia Fotografica, Milan 78, 78, 85, 10, 111, 129. Patrick Taylor 96b